REFLECTIONS
AT THE
SALT MONUMENT

Volume I: Songs and Contemplations
(1997 - 2002)

MARGOT WEISS

Library of Congress Catalog Number to be assigned

ISBN 0-9654470-5-7

Sephiran Press
8725 N. 87th Street
Longmont, CO 80503

The Salt Monument
P. O. Box 1542
Boulder, CO 80306
email: saltmonument@hotmail.com

≈

This book is dedicated to you...

As one grain of salt to another,

TABLE OF CONTENTS

ONE HAND

The signature of humanity—
Throughout all time, all places, all peoples.

~

PREFACE

The Salt Monument is an inexplicable and ineffable experience. Some of those who have experienced it know how even a single encounter with the Monument can provoke irrevocable realizations about being human. For those who have not, there is no amount of words or description that can convey its utterly unique and unexpected impact.

To commemorate the fifth anniversary of the daily world births and deaths observance, the present volume is a compilation of writings between the years 1997 and 2002. In the story of what may one day come to be known as a world heritage, *Reflections at the Salt Monument, Volume I* is an historic document of the very infancy of the Monument.

Like the Salt Monument, this book has evolved in an organic, unpremeditated way—not with the intention of being a book but more as a series of snapshots, each written in the exigency of a moment, whether of grief, awe, ecstasy, outrage, perplexity...As such, there are many things this book is *not*. It is not a book to read quickly nor from cover-to-cover. It is not even a book to *read*, but rather a book to *feel* and be felt deeply, even perhaps over years. This book is *not* designed as a comprehensive or balanced commentary on, for instance, death, our world, or children, *or* the Salt Monument. It is quite simply an anthology of some writings during this five-year period, arranged in retrospect by themes, not chronologically, in a somewhat random order. Dates are included for reference. This book is *not* a pleasant book to read. The picture it paints is neither pretty nor optimistic; nor does it herald an eminent era of heightened consciousness.

Reflections is uncomfortably rooted in much of what we do not want to face: the grippingly-poignant enormity of suffering, poverty, cruelty, negligence, and complicity in our world; the incomprehensible and overwhelming actuality of humanity, life, time, our planet, our universe…It is a glimpse of the exquisite, the terrible, the undeniable. Its scope is vast, necessarily incomplete, and discomfiting.

This having been said, this book is ultimately a series of reflections on compassion, kindness, dignity, peace, reverence, love, and the mystery of all.

For myself, in my daily dedication, I have found: no matter how many days I have sat at the Salt Monument, I have yet to even marginally plumb its depths, explore its wisdom, realize its magnitude. I accept how insufficiently this volume bears witness to the true enormity of the Salt Monument. Even with all these words, there is so much—so incalculably much—that is not said. Nevertheless, at the dawning of the Salt Monument, I submit these writings as an offering to extend our caring, unsettle our ingrained awareness, and expand our perspectives.

~

One Hand: The Signature Of Humanity

One Hand is:

~ The mysterious sign humans have left on rocks around the world from 40,000 years ago to present.

~ A universal symbol of humanity.

~ A tribute to all humans throughout all time.

~ A declaration of presence.

~ The love expressed in human touch.

~ A depiction of being human with no distinction of race, gender, economics, age, culture.

~ Evidence of the unique self-awareness and symbolic creativity of human consciousness.

~ The signature of every human being.

~ An expression of the impermanence and evanescence of life.

~ A reminder of our truly common denominator: we *all* have a human body.

~ A dedication to the whole human body, the body of humanity.

~ A universal greeting.

~ An appeal to peace.

~ A mark of timelessness.

~ The human hand—primary agent of human ingenuity.

~ The essence—the spirit—of being human, not the literal or manifest but the trace.

~ The precious gift of embodiment.

~ A philosophical assertion: what is *not there* is the subject.

~ An emblem of the unity of all humankind.

~ A prayer for humans to tread lightly on our planet, to leave a faint imprint.

~ An entreaty to make of our hands (twelve-billion-plus hands) one hand.

~ The classic Zen koan: "the *sound* of one hand."

~ Testimony to the human sense of mystery, beauty, creativity.

December 1999

~

THE DAILY CEREMONY

The daily ceremony at The Salt Monument engages us in a series of thoughts and images, keyed by music, relating to the family of humanity. Accustomed as we are to our differences and distinctions, here we focus rather on that which unites us and is undeniably universal—not as conceptual ideas, but as actuality. The following guidepost to the daily observance at the Salt Monument provides some starting points for contemplation at each of the passages we will visit in the stream of life.

There really are over six billion individual human lives being lived today, right this moment—every person with a name, a unique face, and their own heroic journey, navigating as best they can through life's joys and sorrows, trials and blessings. We are all living the same day, every day, one day at a time. For some, it is now morning. For others, midnight. Yet together we are all breathing, right now...in and out...in and out. The ceremony at the Salt Monument is a journey of communion with the family of humanity.

HARP SONG
A brief, spontaneous harp and vocal song has become a daily tradition.

DEDICATION   [Spoken in the universal first person]
In joy, solemnity, and awe, I place myself here in the symbolic presence of all of humanity. Bringing my own concerns, I offer what is personal to me to be transfigured into what is universal to all. To do this, I need not expect or pressure myself to be suddenly pure and altruistic. With only the *intent* to think of others, I start

wherever I am, right now—whether tired, angry, happy, worried, ill, reverent, overwhelmed...wherever I am at this moment. Here, at the Salt Monument, I will find millions—even *hundreds of millions*—of people who share a similar experience with me. Thus, and simply, from my own individual story, my personal self begins to expand in vivid awareness of so many others. Acknowledging it is unattainable, yet still, I offer myself in loving attention to honor and recognize every individual person alive today. I here open my heart and soul as wide and deeply as I am able, to dissolve myself in the sea of humanity.

WE ARE ALL HERE NOW

If we were to take a drop of you—your blood or sweat or a tear—and let it evaporate, we would have a grain of salt which had come from your individual living body. If we could collect and evaporate such a drop from *every* person alive today and gather all those grains of salt together, we would have the mass of salt currently before us. The Salt Monument would then literally hold a bodily part of each member of humanity. Every day, when any person was born, we would need to take a drop from their newborn body to add their grain of salt to the Monument. Every day, when any person died, we would take that grain of salt which had come from their body and dissolve it in water. Of course, this is not only impractical but impossible; the Salt Monument therefore does this symbolically.

The Salt Monument is a place where *every*one is included…where *every*one counts...whoever and wherever we are, whatever our circumstances. No matter how glorified or forsaken, miserable or joyous, vile or useless we may feel—there is a place where we are included, we are accepted, we are honored. For every person who is born, there is a greeting of welcome and hope. For every person as they die, there is a blessing of farewell and gratitude. Impossible as it may seem, the Salt Monument is ultimately dedicated to every individual human being who has ever lived, who is alive today, and who will live and die henceforth.

The dream...of peace, equality, freedom, and dignity for all...lives on within us.

OUR GREAT AND GLORIOUS EARTH
Let us realize the reality of our magnificent planet. Huge, to us. Spherical. Suspended in blackness. Always exactly half lit. Majestically rolling us into day and night, turning us around to our seasons, ceaselessly traversing this tiny year-route in the vast darkness of space. Here is the home of every single human being, the home of countless living beings. Let us see ourselves in true perspective of the trillions of other creatures, the billions of Earth years, the untold light-years of our Universe. Let us contemplate the ineffable miracles and mysteries of Earth, and witness the water, the clouds, and the ever-so-thin, day-blue veil of our atmosphere. Let us visit the azure oceans and fiery deserts, the towering mountains and verdant forests, the steamy equator and frozen poles—one light, one dark; and everywhere, everywhere, the endless creativity of life. Let us ask ourselves, truly...Could it be *more* beautiful?

THE *EVERYONE* MEDITATION
For this passage, we will choose something that every single person did or experienced at some time during the 24-hour period of a day. We will then focus intently on seeing or vividly witnessing as many of the more than six billion individuals doing that as we possibly can. During this instrumental, which lasts only three minutes, we will each immerse ourselves in a veritable barrage of images, a torrential montage of split-second impressions. The objective is to see as many people as clearly as possible. Most important is the attempt to include at least one representative of every conceivable sector of humans—spanning all ages, locations, possibilities. Be sure to include *all* actual experiences; not just what is

pleasant and familiar, but also that which may be strange, heart-breaking, and even horrid. Without censure, let us look simply upon what is. The impossibility of this exercise is, of course, inherent: It would mean clearly visualizing over 35 million people each second! Yet, earnestly approaching this meditation will yield a profoundly expanded glimpse of humanity.

Our Thoughts Are With You

Here we will direct our thoughts to some of the people on this day who are suffering circumstances of great difficulty or common hardship. We might, for example, choose to focus on: those who are hopelessly hungry today, or the millions of homeless refugees; people surrounded by violent conflict or devastated by a recent tragedy...or those who are ill...mercilessly oppressed...alone...impoverished. During this passage, we will bring heartful, vivid awareness to the actual reality which these people are living—today, tomorrow, yesterday, perhaps even every day of their entire lives.

In Remembrance

Today is the anniversary of thousands upon thousands of years, and billions upon billions of births and deaths, tragedies and celebrations. The mandala formed in the turning bowl of dissolved salts represents those who have come and gone before us. Drawn into the dissolution of time and individual identity, we see: the distinctions by which we define ourselves...our accomplishments and struggles in which we are so absorbed...the treasures of life we cherish—all these dissolve with time. The once illustrious, the heinous, the anonymous, the unheralded billions—all are now, equally, gone. We turn our thoughts to our loved ones who have passed away, to the generations upon generations of our relatives, to the countless ancestors of humanity—all of whose contributions bring us here today. We now bear their dreams, their wounds, their burdens, their gifts. We here greet in gratitude and remembrance the unknown billions upon billions who have come and gone, come and gone...over thousands upon thousands of years... Passing through...We are *all* just passing through.

In Honor Of Those Who Died Today

On the day each of us dies, we will be honored at the Salt Monument as one tiny grain of salt dissolving in water. Today it was *not* you or me—but for over 150,000 people this day was of the utmost significance as they each exhaled the last breath of their life. Some died in peace and with loved ones. Some died alone; some in agony. Many were aged and ready for death. Some died unexpectedly. Some were very young. Let us look with love and gratitude into the eyes of each of the multitude whose life ends today, and let us stand together in awe before the great mystery of death, which we each face.

For some of the many of us, now left here today without a loved one, this day is forever filled with grief and poignancy. During our lifetime, we shall each come to know the sorrow of loss—we are joined here in mourning. If, for each person who died somewhere in the world today, a loved one came forward with a single grain of salt to place in this water, saying simply, "My father died today...It was my child...my mother...my beloved...my friend...my grandparent..."—if just one of each of the grieved came to the Salt Monument to honor their loved one, we would see a line of humanity from this doorway stretching fully twenty-five miles. We extend our hearts to each of you.

The last mound of salt to be dissolved in the sacrament today represents the 25,000 to 32,000 children under the age of five who died today, as every day, due to causes related to poverty. Let us hold each of these children to our hearts as we join in their last breath.

SILENCE

Let us join together for a few moments of silence and stillness.

WELCOME TO THOSE BORN TODAY

On any given day, there are about 100 million people floating, nearly weightless, inside the watery darkness of another human being. The only world these people live and grow in for nine uninterrupted months is very different than the world they (and we) are born into. Let us visit the world of the floating people—the unborn. "I come forth from the dark, fluid, inner world of a rhythmic heart, to a world which *you* call *the* world."

On this day, nearly 360,000 of these people emerged through the great doorway of skin to inhale a breath of this air for the first time, as we all once did. They will now breathe in and out, again and again, as you and I do, for the rest of their lives, however long that may be. We here honor and bless our newborn children—their pilgrimage through the birth canal, their first breath, the first touch of love, their naming. We pause with these grains of salt for a flower blessing, that our newborns' first glimpse of our world may be of the beauty and miracle of this planet. Silently in love, we greet these people: Welcome to our world.

Again, if we were to imagine a line of people—this time each mother holding her newborn child of today—bringing a single grain of salt to add to the Salt Monument, that line would extend over sixty-five miles. Let us be *realistic* in our blessings and welcome to these, our newest children: Nearly every child born today (more than nine out of ten) lives in a *less developed country,* where they will face perilous conditions of poverty, malnutrition, disease, violence, and early mortality that most of us cannot even imagine.

If you ever meet a person anywhere in the world whose birthday is today's date, you can say, "I was thinking of you the day you were born. I am so glad to finally meet you."

What if, as a world family, we pledged ourselves as parents do, to every one of our newborn of today?

> If you are hungry, we will feed you.
> If you are cold, we will warm you.
> If you are sick, we will care for you.
> If you are in danger, we will protect you.
> If you are happy, we will delight with you.
> If you have a dream, we will help you.
> If you are victorious, we will celebrate with you.
> If you have something to say, we will listen.
> If you call, we will answer.

THE GIFT OF LOVED ONES

In the context of billions, we can see how exceptional our contact with others truly is. Even those who we merely pass once— unknown and in transit—are among the very few with whom we will ever have contact. Even fewer people we truly know. Our loved ones are a rare treasure in a world of unseen billions who we will never encounter. Let us visit with people around the world in the cherished circles of dear ones—the love and hope for our children; the blessing of grandparents, parents, and family members; the chance to share a lifetime with a beloved partner; the joy of close friends.

How precious and rare are those very few in life who we know as loved ones. We share this with each of the six billion who are in turn blessed with their own loves. We are a gift to one another— within the eons of space and the silence of time, forever and always, we are a gift to one another.

ONE HAND

Imagine if, every day at the same moment all around the world, we were to take a global *roll call*—"Raise your hand if you are here today!"—and every one of over six billion people, whoever and wherever they were, whatever their circumstances, each waved their hand into the air as an expression of their inclusion in the human family. *"I am here!"*

Let us reach through time and space to celebrate the unity of humanity. May we greet one another anew, in wonder—treasuring our contact, restoring our honor for one another. Reaching out together as one hand, we touch those who have gone before us, those who are breathing along with us today, and those who will come and go in the eons to come. May each and every one of us realize true joy and fulfillment.

THE MONUMENT ITSELF

*The Salt Monument is a place
where everyone is included...
where everyone counts...
whoever and wherever we are,
whatever the circumstances.*

~

Why The Salt Monument?

Many people ask: Where did the idea of the Salt Monument come from?

Sometime in the late 1980's, in one of those sweeping moments of love for all of humanity which stirs in so many of us, the idea of the Salt Monument was born. I do not recall the actual moment. I felt that love and I wondered:

How many individual people are there really? What is it to truly love each and every one of over five billion people [the world population at that time]? How can I be sure to forget *no one*? How many really is five billion? What does five billion of something look like?

In that instant, I wondered simply: What if each person was represented as one grain of salt?

The idea stayed with me as a question, but it wasn't until December, 1991 that I took the first and necessary step: counting individual grains of salt in order to figure the total mass. The experience was unforgettable. At the time, I wrote: "The salt population model does exactly what I foresaw, but it is more unnerving than I could have possibly anticipated. Painstakingly and awestruck, I meticulously counted out 2,700 grains of salt (the smallest measure I could find). It took almost two hours. In the process I was amazed at how many grains were in the smallest pinch—how 1,000 or 2,000 looked like almost nothing. Using the 2,700 measure, I calculated the fill to a container that held 330,000, and from there I got to two million. When I got to the truth of the 5.3 billion, I felt practically sickened. As miniscule and unnoticeable as 1,000 or 2,000 grains are, to get to 5.3 billion, would be about 1,500 pounds of salt! The volume is truly inconceivable. And that each tiny, almost unnoticeable grain—each one in 1,500 pounds of salt—represents a person alive today! It was so cataclysmic. I was stunned, altered, shaken."

Nearly six years later I decided to actually build the Salt Monument. On September 17, 1997 (a date I will never forget), I enacted the first daily world births and deaths ceremony. I have done this every day since then. It has profoundly affected me.

Why the Salt Monument? The present and future magnitude of our population is implicated in every single concern of today and tomorrow, yet this goes largely unnoticed because of our scale and perspective. The Salt Monument creates a graphic encounter with incomprehensible and unseen realities.

Further still, the Salt Monument is a sorely needed symbol of unity and universal love for all humankind. At the Salt Monument, we are each simply and profoundly one human being among many others. In the simplicity of its presence, we are wordlessly impressed with the most fundamental realities of human existence…birth, life, death.

Why the Salt Monument? Because it is an idea whose time has come.

March 1999

~

To The Human Body

I am building the Salt Monument because when I send my daily prayers to my human family, I want to include everyone. Many people will die today—some peacefully and graciously, others alone and forgotten; some by cruelty or famine, others unjustly, or untimely. Their deaths will profoundly affect many more people. Many people will enter the world today—some loved and nurtured; others unloved, unfortunate, and without an adequate opportunity to grow and thrive. A billion people or more will wake at their dawn today to a life in which they feel they do not matter—a life of hopelessness, drudgery, suffering, oppression, hunger, torment. When I say my prayers today, I want to include everyone—those who feel important and fortunate, and those many more who do not. I want at least for a brief moment each day to send one simple prayer of love to the *human body*.*

The Salt Monument is a tool to say this prayer. It creates a focus and a visceral (not mental or conceptual) representation of the entire human body. I want to share this prayer, this tool with as many people as have eyes to see and ears to hear.

October 1998

*I use this term as an alternate to *humanity*. Humanity seems somehow disembodied. In the parallel I am using, it is akin to what we refer as a "student body." It puts the bodies into the reference. It sees a particular grouping, in this case human beings, as constituting an actual trans-body, a body which functions as a whole.

~

Why Salt?

Salt is a universal constituent of every human body. If we were to take a drop of blood or sweat or a tear from any person and let it evaporate, we would have a grain of salt which had come from that person's individual living body. Salt has been chosen as the representative element for humanity for many other symbolic, historical, and philosophical reasons:

Salt is a naturally occurring, abundantly plentiful, organic crystal on Earth, found on every continent and in every ocean.

The ocean within us—our blood, sweat, and tears—has the same saltiness as the Precambrian seas from which life began three billion years ago. Salt is absolutely requisite to *all* life on the planet—whether single cells or complex organisms. Salt is essential to human life—muscle contractions, nerve impulses, cellular health, even the very beating of our hearts, all depend on the presence of salt.

Because it is so necessary to life, every culture throughout time has deep traditions related to salt—it has affected history, philosophy, and religion, and inspired vast folklore; it has been woven into language and has even served as money. The well-known biblical phrase, *salt of the earth*, refers to salt as a symbol of simplicity and universality.

Specific to the meaning of the Salt Monument, the formation of salt crystals via the evaporation of ocean water can be symbolically related to birth; the uniqueness and yet similarity of each crystal resembles the paradox of both our individual uniqueness and similarity; and the solubility of salt in water has a symbolic parallel to the dissolution of the body in death.

November 1997

~

REALITIES AND QUESTIONS *FIRST*, NOT ANSWERS

It may be frustrating to some people that the Salt Monument doesn't provide us with solutions to our problems and questions. We have become accustomed in this culture to people presenting us with the answers: the five-steps (or however many) to solution, the program that some individual or group has ingeniously and proudly come up with to save the day simultaneous with their declaring that the day needs to be saved.

Before we can come up with answers, however, we need to know what are our *questions*. We need to become fully and accurately aware of basic principal realities amongst our family on our planet today. The questions themselves are complex, multi-dimensional, and interdependent.

But who wants to hear about problems without answers? No one in this country/culture/lifestyle really wants to hear me talking about how many people (especially halfway across the world) are starving today, how many are oppressed and tormented, how many children are diseased and impoverished, how three billion people don't have access to basic waste sanitation, how brutal violence brings death daily to tens of thousands, how we are responsible for the gross exploitation of people and environments around the world in order to have our modern conveniences…and more and more. Who wants to think about these things?! It's too upsetting! We don't want to be upset. We don't want to be faced with unpleasantness and irresolvability. Who wants to feel their own hypocrisy, greed, ignorance, indifference and shame, and further have no way to escape from it? We prefer to hide, to delude ourselves, to entertain ourselves, to stuff ourselves senseless, to engage in personal growth, to play with ever more sophisticated technologies, to humor ourselves with minuscule gains in environmental awareness, to grow richer, to do anything...*anything* but *not* see, think, talk, and certainly not *feel*, all those upsetting things. Maybe one little angle on it from one person or one organization is acceptable. We all know that UNICEF is going to hit on us about the desperate conditions of children around the world, so that becomes permissible. And their appeal is easily answered: either throw the literature away quickly before you really read it and feel it, or write them a check—then you've done your part and you can return to your self-absorbed comforts absolved of guilt.

But to be a simple person, talking about these unpleasant realities from *many* perspectives that are virtually undeniable and not having any solution or any request for money to solve it...this is simply too much. It's too overwhelming. If we do let it in, then we come to that wall of helplessness, hopelessness, and impotence. We are begging for solutions. We want answers to help alleviate our uneasiness with the discomforting perspectives.

It is not time for answers yet. We need to see the questions first. Questions like: What is our responsibility to our global family? To future generations? What is the role of compassion? How can we silently consent to the gaping inequities between us? And many more.

The Salt Monument is unique in that it not only doesn't present an answer, it also does not have an opinion. It is designed to merely reflect what is: this is how many, this is what is happening, this is what is...

How disturbing.

June 1998

~

How Many *Is* Six Billion?

Have you ever wondered how many six billion people really is? Sometimes models can bring comprehensibility to ungraspable ideas. A simple pen and paper exercise can vividly demonstrate the current magnitude of the human population.

What if I make a dot by pressing my pen on a paper, saying, "This dot represents one human being." Let's say I very rapidly and consistently make five dots every second. Try it; it is possible but it is very fast. If I were to do that *every* hour of *every* day until I made one dot for every person alive today—how long do you think it would take me to finish? Make some dots on your own piece of paper and think about it. By my tone, you may already understand that the answer to this is going to be astonishing. Make an estimate before you read on.

Now, let's write out the mathematics of it.

To make just *one billion* dots at the rate of five dots per second would take:

200,000,000 seconds; which equals
3,333,333 minutes; which equals
55,555 hours; which equals
2,315 days; which equals
6.34 years!

It would take me over six years to just make *one* billion dots— working at it *every* single second of *every* single day for over six years! That means it would take thirty-eight years for me to make one dot for every person alive today!

Of course, I could never actually complete this project in my lifetime, even if I dedicated every second to it because I would be outpaced by the seventy million or so additional people per year that were added during each of the thirty-eight years I was busy making all those dots.

How can any of us truly relate to "all of humanity?" The truth is: the number of us is utterly overwhelming and incomprehensible.

January 1998

~

O GREAT AND WONDROUS TEACHER—
TO THE SALT MONUMENT

When you instructed me to build your body,
I had no idea what you would do.
Although I *thought* I knew how profound you were,
I see now, I knew nothing, *nothing* of your great splendor,
Your infinite wisdom,
Your profound and subtle teachings.
Every day you bring me deeper,
Yet now I understand: you are unfathomable.
Utterly unfathomable.

I could sit beneath you every day of my life,
With fully rapt attention,
And yet still I would not complete the lessons you have to teach.

Even further,
The longer you exist,
The more…even more…
You will have to offer us,
Containing not only our recent present and near future,
But our recent past and past futures as well.

O Wondrous Teacher,
Will any other than me
Experience even the small part of your Great Teaching?
Life, birth, death, time, cycles, individuality, humility, awareness,
Insignificance, humanity, compassion, equality, transcendence…

O Great and Wondrous Teacher!
I sit before you,
Ever humbled,
Ever in awe
Of your magnitude, gravity, perfection, and grace.

I am honored to serve you.
For this, I am eternally grateful.

August 1999

~

THE COLOR OF SALT

An individual grain of salt is a *clear*, cubic crystal which *appears* starkly white when viewed from a distance and in a grouping. Some people may wonder: If we are representing all of humanity, all of whom come in many varying skin colors, why not use a substance of various colors? Everyone is not *white*. In fact, as the Salt Monument graphically and unforgettably demonstrates in the perspective exhibits, the <u>vast</u> majority (more than 90%) of humanity is *of color*! Yet, if we compare a presumably *white* person's skin to the color of salt, we will clearly see there is no correlation. No one's skin is the color of salt. The usage of the term *white* for a person is inaccurate and has arisen as a discriminatory term. Besides, the appearance of the color of our epidermis is one of the most superficial and least enduring aspects of our physical bodies.

The blood of every human being is red. The bones of every human being are white. The tears of every human being are salty.

To focus on our humanity—the very purpose of the Salt Monument— we must go deeper, *much deeper*, than external appearances. We must go deeper than the surface differences not only of skin color, but also the equally superficial distinctions of age, gender, occupation, beliefs, possessions, and more. None of these differentiations universally define us as human beings. We have focused on such differences for millennium. They have not, they do not, they will not, bring unity because they focus on disparity. We have many ways to categorize ourselves. Our diversity is evident, deserving of celebration and the teachings of tolerance. Yet what happens when we counterbalance our habitual recognition of our *dissimilarities* with the equally valid representation of our *similarities*?

At the core of every person's body is a frame of bones, closer in color to salt than anyone's skin and far more enduring. If you examine the remains of a million people around the world, of whatever skin color and whether from a million years ago or five hundred or fifty, you will find only their skeletons—their *white* bones.

Scrape a few beads of sweat from the brow of any person in the world; let it dry and you will have a crystal or two of salt. Gather a few tears of sorrow as they fall from the eyes of any person on the planet—whatever their skin color, their age, their nationality, their religion, their economic status, their gender. When the water has evaporated, a white crystal of salt will remain. Distill the blood or urine of any person, and salt crystals will appear.

It is time for us to find ways to embrace our *human beingness*, in addition to our *unlikeness*. To recognize our similarities, along with our dissimilarities. To celebrate our connectedness, instead of our separation. To acknowledge our inner depth, rather than external appearances.

February 1999

~

When The World Comes To The Salt Monument

When the world knows about the Salt Monument, it will become a place where people from all around the world, of all cultures, traditions, and beliefs come to say *their* prayers, to sing *their* songs, to practice *their* rituals of love and peace for all humanity. Everyone has such prayers/songs/rituals. Every culture has a ritual of welcome to the newborn and of farewell to the dead. Every belief, at its deepest core (beyond sectarianism), touches on the universal ideals of love and peace for all humanity.

When anyone comes to the Salt Monument, it is natural for them to want to express their feeling in their own tradition. And unlike anything ever before, the Salt Monument is so completely neutral, people of each and every tradition can engage in their own expression equally. I believe there may one day be so many cultural offerings at the Salt Monument, they will be scheduled for every possible hour of every day. That is all people will need to do, i.e. schedule it—we would like to sing, we would like to play music, we would like to meditate, we would like to say these prayers, ad infinitum.

If I live to see this, I will watch and witness in joy as I did last week (when one visitor came and conducted his own celebration.) Although what I witness may not be the way *I* feel the Salt Monument the most powerfully, I will sit in the ecstasy that the Salt Monument has provided a place for someone else to feel it as they do. This is the true beauty of the Monument: it can be exactly what and how anyone wants. Everyone can create their own experience of it.

The Salt Monument will give everyone a place to honor and express in their own way their universal love for all humankind.

August 1999

~

One Day You Will...
TO THE SALT MONUMENT

One day you will have an exquisite building
And a warm room all of glass
With views of great trees and flowers,
Water and life, clouds and air,
Stars, Moon, and Sun.

One day there will always be someone sitting
In vigil with you,
Every minute of every day,
Holding a place of love and honor
For each and every person on Earth.

One day people from all cultures
Will come to conduct their
Ceremonies, songs, and prayers
To all humanity.
They will devote sacred gifts to honor you
And you will be surrounded by a
Great circle of stones from around the world
Speaking of peace in every human language.

One day you will have all this and more
As a tribute to you,
Our great Monument to Humanity.

Until then,
I try my humble best to do justice to your greatness.
I hope one day
I will be able to witness
All this and more
That you so truly deserve.

I look forward to this
For you and all of us.
One day.

October 1999

~

The Global Village and The Salt Monument

It has been recognized that wherever, whenever, and whoever it is, humans tend to organize naturally in what we call a *village* or *tribal* setting. Usually these groupings range from twenty to five hundred to be optimally functional. Of course, larger conglomerations of villages or tribes often function together as well, these being called *nations*. If we lived in a small village centuries ago, or in a small town eighty years ago, or in an indigenous setting today, we would be aware of who was born, who died, and how everyone was doing. We would have ceremonies and gatherings, symbols and traditions to acknowledge this. This is universal in all cultures, no matter who, where, or when.

Of course the Salt Monument is the natural progression of such practices within the scope of what has been referred to as the *global village*. This is a simple and convincing way to explain the Salt Monument. It is easy to comprehend, pertinent to our times, and has the social/spiritual/unifying implications already imbedded in the analogy.

March 1999

In Our Greatest Hope and Deepest Sorrow

The Salt Monument stands at the juncture of people's greatest hope (universally represented in the birth of the newborn) and of people's deepest sorrow (in grieving the death of a loved one). When the Salt Monument is serving its function to humanity, it will be the place where people will come to celebrate, to grieve, and to realize.

There are four great (and common) passages in life when people will especially be drawn to the Salt Monument:

~ During pregnancy, they will bring their unborn child to the Salt Monument, to prepare for the birth, to see the child's place in our family, to comprehend the great daily birthing of which they will one day soon be a participant;

~ Newborn infants and children will be brought by parents to the Salt Monument, to witness the family each child has just joined, to experience the enormity of individual humans alive now, to stand in awe of the passage of life one day at a time for each human being;

~ The aged who know it is almost time to go will come to the Salt Monument, to fully realize their mortality, to see their place in the flow of life and time, to bring reality and perspective to their individual life, to rejoice at the continuum;

~ Those who are mourning the death of a loved one will come to the Salt Monument, to share the reality of their grief with the family of humanity.

Of course, many people who are not at such momentous life events will also be drawn to the Salt Monument. We will come to the Salt Monument when we have experienced some realization of: the oneness of humanity, the singleness of our planet, the issues/

concerns caused by human rights, and more. We will come to the Salt Monument when we want to petition humanity to put an end to hunger, poverty, and war. We will come to the Salt Monument to share our anguish and despair at the random injustice of fate. We will come to the Salt Monument…

There are six billion reasons to come to the Salt Monument.

The first unborn child visited the Salt Monument on August 22. It was a remarkable event for me, both because it was the first occasion of what I believe will be a tradition in the future, and because the idea of a conscious yet unborn person walking around via another person's body vehicle is simply astounding. I laid hands on the mother and communed with the fetal person (six months womb-old) as if I had just discovered the mystical miracle of pregnancy and birth. And so the first unborn at the Salt Monument has had its historic first.

The other day, someone said she wanted to ask me a question. She told of their friends, whose two-year-old son died suddenly just last week. Sick from a fever the night before, the mother came to him in the morning and found him having a hard time breathing. She held him in her arms, and suddenly his body simply went limp. He was dead long before any emergency help was even called. She wanted to ask if this couple could come to the Salt Monument as part of their grieving process. I cried in hearing the story. I wept at the Salt Monument that day and the next in feeling their grief and that of all parents whose children die. It happens in one moment; the sorrow and re-experiencing of it lasts an entire lifetime. There is no way to forget such an event. This is where life gets real, gets personal, gets serious, and too seems so unfair and inexplicable. The request alone incredibly deepened my own experience at the Salt Monument.

This is why there is a Salt Monument.

One day, when the Salt Monument is known and in public location(s), there may be hundreds of grieving people who come to weep and acknowledge their loss. On the same day, also there will be hundreds of hopeful new parents with their unborn and infants and young children who come to celebrate the regeneration of life. On that same day, there will also be: aged people coming to say goodbye to life and all of the living; holy people coming to bring a prayer of love and peace to all humanity; activists and leaders coming to comprehend the realities of the human world; thoughtful people considering their actual relation to humankind and time; and more and more.

Every day, sometime in the future, there will be people of every age, ranging in deep and real feelings from awe, to joy, to sorrow, to realization, to compassion, and more—all together at the same time at the Salt Monument. Some people who would otherwise have hated each other may find themselves crying next to and with their presumed enemy, united by grief. While some are crying, children will be laughing. We will be all together in the magic and pathos, the mystery and reality, of life. We will experience a deep and unforgettable contemplation of life.

When all this happens one day, the Salt Monument will be fulfilling its great purpose.

September 1999

~

THE SALT PERSPECTIVE

Keeping things in perspective—

Ourselves as individuals;
Ourselves as a species on this planet at this moment in time;
The infinite enormity of the mysterious microcosmos;
Our existence in an incomprehensibly vast universe;

—Is increasingly difficult amidst the modern profusion of information and our personal absorption.

Using the simple symbol of a crystal of salt as a starting point,
The salt perspective engages us in an exploration of
Dimensional context and relative scale.

It is hard to comprehend there are nearly six billion people, especially spread out on a sphere that is nearly 200 million square miles. The salt perspective can help us picture it. When we travel in an airplane at an altitude of 30,000 feet and look down upon the landscape, we see structures and roads as miniaturized evidence of human activity. But from that distance, a human being appears incredibly small—perhaps the size of a single grain of salt. Imagine if, at that altitude, we were to take every human being on the planet, represent each one as a grain of salt, and gather them together in one grouping. We would end up with about a cubic yard (27 cubic feet) of tiny grains of salt. Perhaps to so reduce humanity and render us inanimate seems unfamiliar, but it allows an unlimited extension of understanding.

We have, for example, grown accustomed to the reduction of our huge, life-filled Earth into an inert, fourteen-inch ball. A *globe* has become a familiar model of our planet, which simultaneously fulfills a virtually endless array of applications.

So it is with the Salt Monument as a model of the human race. In a series of interactive exhibits and examples of scale which accompany the monument, we can explore understandings and perspectives otherwise incomprehensible to us. For example:

Our body: If a grain of salt represented one cell of our body, it would take about ten thousand Salt Monuments filled to the current level to represent the sixty trillion cells which make up one human body.

Life on Earth: If every grain of salt in the Salt Monument today stood for one year, this would represent about the number of years the Earth has been a planet. Find the two billion marker on the cube. That would represent when single-cell life first emerged on Earth. Find the four billion marker on the cube. That would represent when sponges—the first multi-cellular life— began. Find the 4.5 billion marker on the cube. That would represent the first appearance of human–type creatures. One-quarter cup of salt would represent the past 350,000 years of human life on Earth, long before recorded history. Less than one teaspoon of all the salt currently in the Salt Monument would represent the 10,000 years of known human history in the context of the history of the Earth.

Our galaxy: If a grain of salt represented our Sun or any average star, the next nearest star would be another tiny, grain of salt fully *nine* miles away! It would take about forty Salt Monuments filled to the current level to represent the number of suns or stars in our galaxy, the Milky Way. To model the size of our Milky Way, we could take that 68,000 pounds of salt and spread those 24,000,000,000 individual grains throughout a circle that was 210,000 miles in diameter.

August 1997

~

TECHNICAL SPECIFICS

The Salt Monument measures 9.5 feet high (2.9 m) and 7.5 feet (2.3 m) wide and deep. The four foot (1.2 m) cube has an interior area of 64 cubic feet (1.8 cubic meters) and is made of 3/4" (2 cm) plexiglass. It was fabricated and engineered by the Denver plant of an international plastics company. Completely empty, the cube itself weights about 450 pounds (204 k). The necessary thickness of the material was determined based on engineering calculations rendered by licensed structural engineers. Factors of tensile, flexural, and compressive strength given the weight and density of the salt were taken into account. The Salt Monument is engineered to hold up to 4,000 pounds (1,800 k) of salt, which would represent over 14 billion people—far more than even the highest population estimates. It is expected that a slight, but structurally harmless, deflection of the cube faces may occur if it holds over 3,000 pounds (1,400 k) of salt. Interestingly, the bonded edges of the cube are actually stronger than the faces.

The uppermost corner of the pivoted cube houses two tetrahedrons, which form the opening for filling and cleaning the Salt Monument, as well as for adding the daily births. (A tetrahedron is a three-dimensional figure with four triangular faces; in both of the Salt Monument tetrahedrons, three faces are solid and the fourth is open.) The *apex tetrahedron* (at top) swivels on a plastic dowel and is opened by magnet. The *birth tetrahedron* (inside) has a funneled 1/16" (1.6 mm) hole drilled into it, to allow for the slowest possible free-flowing stream of the birth salt.

At the bottom corner of the pivoted cube is the *death exit*, controlled by a precision, adjustable, ball valve. This opening serves for taking out the daily deaths.

The cube was completed in December, 1998. Refinements were made during January, 1999. Testing was conducted during February and the first filling of the Salt Monument was completed in March, 1999. Although the daily world births/deaths have been conducted every day beginning September 17, 1997, the observance has occurred at the actual, completed Monument every day since March, 1999.

The base is made of 2-inch (5 cm) square tubular steel, and itself weights about 200 pounds (90 k). It was welded and powder-coated by local firms in Boulder County. The upper triangle of the base, on which three faces of the cube rest in the pivoted position, supports the enormous weight of the Monument by virtue of matching the angle of the cube at 55 degrees—thus distributing the tonnage. It is estimated that the base could support 10,000 pounds (4,500 k) or more.

Research into what type and grade of salt would be best suited for the monument began in 1997 with the Salt Institute in Washington DC and with Morton Salt at their Chicago headquarters. Numerous sizes and types of salt were tested and measured. In the end, common table salt was selected based on considerations of size, uniformity, cubic form, solubility, availability, familiarity, and cost.

The entire premise of the Salt Monument's mass of salt is based on the average weight of an individual grain of salt multiplied by billions. It should be noted that determining the average weight of a grain of salt is no less daunting than figuring the average weight of a human being from random groupings. Just as people can actually range in weight from three pounds to three hundred, so do grains of salt vary. Some grains of salt are scarcely a speck, while others appear formidable by comparison. Samples of 20, 40, 100, 200, 400, and 1,200 grains of salt were weighed on several different microanalytic scales. Final weigh-ins were conducted by analytic balance specialists on a certified electrobalance scale which measures micrograms, that is, six decimal points of a gram.

Based on these findings, for the purposes of the Monument, the average weight of a single grain of salt was calculated as .1208 milligrams. From this, each 25 pound (11.3 k) bag of salt is estimated to contain about 90 million grains of salt.

The Salt Monument currently holds about 1700 pounds (770 k) of salt, representing the total world population of about 6,245,000,000 (September, 2002). The total weight of the Monument, including the weight of the cube and the base, is thus about 2,400 pounds (1,090 k).

The salt representing the daily births and deaths was initially measured based on weight, using the .1208 milligram/grain figure. For ease of the daily process, i.e. rather than needing to use an analytic scale every day, the volume of those amounts of salt was measured and is used to approximate the daily world births and deaths. About 360,000 people are born each day, which is represented by about 1/4 cup of salt, and about 150,000 people die each day, which is represented by less than an 1/8 cup of salt.

It should be noted that although every effort has been made towards accuracy, the Salt Monument is a *symbolic* representation of population figures. It is not unreasonable to expect a plus-or-minus 10% margin of error in the actual, literal number of grains of salt contained in the Monument.

The most respected and reliable sources of world population information, the International Data Base of the International Programs Center (IPC) at the U.S. Bureau of the Census in Washington DC and the United Nations Population Fund have been utilized for population statistics. The IPC figures are updated and revised twice a year, which the Salt Monument incorporates in its representations. Of course, such statistics on a global scale cannot be precisely exact, but are considered accurate estimates, again with the understanding of a margin of error.

ALL OF US

*There really are over six billion
individual human lives being lived today,
right this moment—every person with a name,
a unique face, and their own heroic journey,
navigating as best they can through life's joys
and sorrows, trials and blessings.*

~

I MAY NEVER KNOW YOU

I may never know you,
But I know you live somewhere,
Waking and sleeping each day,
Sustained by the great wave of breath
Breathing in and out of you
As it breathes in and out of me.

I may never know your name,
But I do not need to, to know
How your heart treasures the calling of your name
By someone who loves you.
I know this,
For I know this of me.

I may never look into your eyes,
But I know you search for meaning and hope
And answers to the why and how of life
As I do.

I may never touch your hand,
But I know you have a living body
Which needs nourishment and water,
Safety and touch,
As I do.

I may never know you,
But I know you cherish and yearn
For freedom and dignity
And the chance to make your dreams come true,
As I do.

I may never know you,
And yet I do.

December 1998

~

WE ARE A GIFT TO ONE ANOTHER

We are a gift to one another—

Whether as parent to child,
   friend to friend,
    beloved to beloved—

We are a gift to one another.

Even in our differences and diversity,
Our contrasts and comparisons,

Within the eons of space
And the silence of time,

Forever and always,

  We are a gift to one another.

April 2000

~

One By One—Breath By Breath

Breathing in, breathing out, breathing in, breathing out.

This is the constant wave upon the shore of life for humans and all animals. Breathing. We are all breathing, together, now…in and out, in and out. We can use the breath to connect us not only to the primordial source of being, but also to connect us to one another. Breathe once in and out. During that time, you and every single living human being has also breathed in and out. During that time, you and every single living breathing creature has also breathed in and out with you.

With the Salt Monument, we can imagine each human being, each grain of salt, each of us, one by one, inhaling and exhaling, now and now and now, and the next minute and the next, on and on. Everyone who is alive today is breathing, now—breathing in and out. All together. We are all doing it all together. It is a wind blowing through each of us, all of us, by which we are sustained and connected. So simple.

Then there are the people for whom *this* breath in or out will be of the utmost importance.

For some, this inhalation is their first. The first breath in this life. The first breath of life can only be an inhalation. We call it: birth. On this day, over 358,000 people breathed in their first breath, as you and I once did. They will now breathe in and out, again and again, as you and I do, for the rest of their lives however long that will be.

For some, this exhalation is their last. The last breath of this life. The last breath of life can only be an exhalation. We call it: death. On this day, over 149,000 people breathed out for their last time, as you and I one day will.

One by one. There is only one way that the wave of life passes in us and through us. One by one. One breath in, one breath out. One by one we are born. One day by one day we live. One by one we die. One by one we come and go.

With each inhalation you breathe, fifteen people somewhere in the world have inhaled their very first breath. The beginning...the beginning of their individual life. Birth. Each time as you exhale, six people somewhere in the world will be exhaling their very last breath. The end of their individual life. Death.

Breathe in: fifteen people born. Breathe out: six people die. Breathe in and out: six billion people breathe with you.

Breathing in and breathing out. First breaths. Last breaths. Coming and going. Staying and breathing. One by one.

January 1998

~

As I Walk

I walk down the quiet lane.

My steps are as those taken just now, somewhere, by someone...

I am an infant taking a first step.

I am an elder, walking in pain and infirmity.

I walk at the funeral procession. I am walking miles to carry my
    family's water.

I am walking in the street of the great metropolis. I am walking in
    the rice paddy.

I am walking in the store filled with thousands of things.

I am walking in the refugee camp to line up for today's food bowl.

I am walking in an office to the next desk. I am walking in the
    prison to my cell.

I am walking with my gun to kill my enemies. I am walking in the
    museum of ancient creations.

I am walking to my wedding altar. I am walking at the Antarctic
    research station.

I am walking in my mind with the legs I no longer have.

I am walking in the desert, in the forest, in the slum, in the boat, in
    the plane, in the mountains.

I am walking in the morning, at midnight, in 100 degree heat, in
    sub-zero dusk, in sunset glory.

I am a monk in walking meditation. I am a child walking to school.

I am the country's leader walking in self-importance and responsibility.

I am walking in the factory to take my brief break.

I am walking. I am walking. I am walking.

Wherever I am, whoever I am, whatever I am doing, there are many
of us walking.

Walking. Breathing. Walking. Breathing.

I think of us, as I walk.

March 1999

~

So Many Hearts, So Many Eyes

I sit before the Salt Monument and realize—
Each, every, grain of salt in this cube represents:

A beating heart.
We are so many hearts pulsing just now.
Every one, with a beating heart.

A pair of eyes.
We are so many pairs of eyes seeing
(And some not.)
What are we seeing, right now?
How many sights? Of love, of horror,
Of dirty cities, of beauty, of…of…of…

A pair of hands.
We are so many pairs of hands.
Touching, creating, killing, giving,
Holding, torturing, writing, praying…

Ah… we are so many pairs of feet
On this Earth.
Walking, working, tired, standing,
Running, crippled, sore.

And mouths.
So many mouths,
Each (hopefully) eating today, and
Talking, singing, screaming, grimacing.

We are even so many anuses
Each (hopefully) shitting today.

What a holy corps of possibility, of miracle,
Of biological functioning!

Each day: Six billion ways!
To feel the beating meaning of rhythm and life.
Each day: Twelve billion chances!
To see the myriad images of light and reflection.
To honor the endless function of hands.
To walk our sacred ball in space.
Each day: Six billion opportunities!
To nourish ourselves with the living bodies of others.
To partake in the grand transformation of matter.

What a society! What an occasion!

November 1999

~

Passing Through

I took a rare hiatus from retreat on Sunday to engage in the world. To voluntarily choose to leave my sanctuary for no reason except that I want to is virtually unheard of. It was truly momentous. It is true, I have had a remarkably long stint of solitude and retreat during this month. On this day, I ventured out with a very particular purpose in mind: to simply sit at the Bookend Café. I had no idea that the summer art fair was happening on the open-air Pearl Street Mall that day, and at first I was overwhelmed by the crowd and all the hubbub. Quickly maneuvering myself into an ideal spot—a choice outdoor table in the best position which happened to be vacated just as I walked up—I settled into my station for loving observation. The circumstances were uniquely ideal: the hot day had clouded over and turned into a pleasant warmth with a quiescent green-foliage-tinged glow; a harpist selling tapes and CDs was just across the walkway from where I sat and miraculously provided an ongoing, live, heartful, exquisite musical accompaniment to my entire experience. I stayed there for three hours as a steady stream of several thousand people passed within a few yards of me, and a hundred or so others hung around the vicinity of my chair.

As soon as I was seated, I was overcome—transported into a transcendent view of humanity. I looked into each person as they passed. It is so hard to be a human being. In those who were adults, I saw a massive array of pride, anguish, fear, anger, woundedness, sorrow, superficiality, boredom, confusion, purposelessness, ignorance, desire, attachment, and egoism. I watched the passing ages of humans: the burdened and disappointed middle-aged; the disillusionment and cynicism of the late middle-aged; the elderly with their distinct knowing that its-almost-time-to-go; the youths full of hope, confidence, and self-absorption; the freedom and innocence of young children; the infants just barely discovering the rudiments of their own bodily processes.

I simply watched, and watched, and watched. Some were from here, some from somewhere else. Some dressed like this, others like that. Some were attractive, some were unattractive. Appearances, appearances. We are so thrown by how things appear.

In the wrinkle of time in which I reside, I saw far beyond appearances.

I saw the long-gone seventy-years ago infants and children who are now aged people—withered and obviously in pain, valiantly walking among the younger generations, certain to be dying within a few years or so. Almost time to go, I smiled to each of them, addressing the inner child still residing within, and honoring their lifetime of days and struggle—almost time to go. I loved them so deeply and resounded the whole truth of life so compassionately, their faces would light up in delight as they met my eyes and my smile as they passed through.

Passing through. We are *all* just passing through. What is *now* will soon be *then*. What *was* was once *now*. Who is old was soon before young. Who is young will so soon be old. It is all a great circle and we the players. We are *all* just passing through. Passing through. There is nothing else to do.

I watched every generation as it passed through, clutching their illusions and delusions. *We are the now generation; we own the world.* Yes, and your successors are already upon you readying for their hour of glory; soon you will be crippled and dying; just the other day in diapers and crying. *We are the hardworking, respon-*

sible ones, glued to our worldly success, self-importance, and cell-phones. Yes, just the other day in diapers too, and even sooner to be snuffed out. *We are the happy, proud parents of this infant.* Yes, soon to be harried parents of a troublesome teen. *We are the happy, playful children.* Yes, and soon you will take on your mantle of ego identity and trudge through your personal life drama in a dream of ignorance.

Perhaps the most special for me is to see my children. Now, [the second anniversary of keeping the daily world births and deaths will be on September 17] every child I see under almost two is someone I consider my child. I smile and look into the eyes of every young child and infant. *Hello, dear one. I was thinking of you on the day you were born. I am so glad to get to see you for the first time. You are so beautiful. My your life be filled with blessings.* Some of them see me and know me immediately, acknowledging our connection with their rapt attention and a loving smile.

I sat and witnessed the procession of life—each person looking for love, acceptance, attention, freedom, happiness, purpose. *Hello, I love you because you are. Are you happy? Have you done what you came here to do? Do you know who you really are?* I was like a guru at the darshan line. Just being there, loving everyone, feeling, sending blessings. Indifferent and detached. Infinitely wise and utterly ignorant.

We are all breathing. Breathing. All together. And eating. Everyone of us has eaten something today. Today, and every day, and every day. Eat, drink, shit, pee. Eat, drink, shit, pee. Eat, drink, shit, pee. Consume, consume, consume, reproduce. This is life…Eventually, with time and exposure, the sacred procession of life began to turn into a lewd parade, and it was time to leave my post.

Passing through. We are *all* just passing through.

Does it seem harsh? Perhaps. And realistic too. It is hard to be human. Admittedly, few of us seem to navigate the journey with genuine peace and joy.

I was overwhelmed with emotion. I looked into over a thousand people's eyes—anyone who was looking, I saw into their eyes. I smiled a blessing to each and every one. At times my tears simply flowed in compassion.

It is good for me to get out and see my people. These are my people. These are a few of the many who I love each day at the Salt Monument, where they are symbolized as single grains of salt. Here they are symbolized as single human bodies. It is so amazing for me to see this. I sat there endlessly speechless just to see a few of the so many people. It is good for me to get out and see my people, my aged, my dying, my children, my infants.

July 1999

~

Anniversaries Of Humankind and Earth

Every day is the anniversary of many, many peoples' births (we call it their *birthday*) and many, many peoples' deaths.

Today I realized: if I consciously begin today to take a few moments each day during the death ceremony in remembrance of *everyone* who has ever died on this date in all the years past, then after one year, every human being who has ever died would have been honored. It is not a farfetched idea. The anniversary of someone's death is a profound date for the people who continue on. There are many people who are deeply affected each and every year for the rest of their lives on the date that someone dear to them died—whether child, spouse, parent, leader, teacher... On any given day, all around the world, there are hundreds of millions, even perhaps a billion (for example upon the anniversary of a famous person's death, such as Gandhi), who will be in remembrance of someone's death on that day. Each year, there are 53 million more first anniversaries of death. And then anniversaries upon anniversaries.

Then too, there are the anniversaries of births. Again, this is quite a significant date to nearly all of us (although a few do not recognize or celebrate birthdays). Almost everyone is very aware of their birth date and makes a point of celebrating it with others. In the birth ceremony at the Salt Monument, we can take a moment to honor every person who was born on that date who is alive today or (if we want to again include every single person from the beginning of humans to now) ever.

So I begin today to honor the history of all birth and death anniversaries.

It should be noted that the Earth has its own anniversaries in its circling our Sun/Star. We call those nodal moments the seasons, the four equinoxes/solstices. A year is a real time frame for the Earth itself. For people, we may get, at the *very* most (and usually *much* less), 120 laps on this circular journey. Let us put this in salt perspective context, using one grain of salt to represent one year, one circle around the Sun. Take a container that holds 100 grains and look at it carefully. This is probably more than how many times *you* will hitch a ride around the Sun on the Earth. Now look at the Salt Monument. That is about how many times the earth has gone around the Sun already! (Give or take a billion grains—i.e. the Earth's age is generally estimated at five billion years, not six.)

Talk about a glaring demonstration of seniority. If we believe in respecting our elders, our Earth truly deserves veneration. Its elder-ness is unsurpassed by anything in our context.

October 1999

~

So Many People

So many people, so many.

Each one wishing for the best in life.
For health and longevity.
For success and fulfillment.
For a peaceful life.

So many people, so many.

Each of the parents wishing the best for their children.
A life of health and happiness.
A better life than their own.

The wishes of youth,
                    of adulthood,
                                of the elderly.

So many people, so many,
All wishing for the best.

September 1999

~

The Unseen Billions: Our Global Family

Combined with our first views of the Earth from space, the increase of worldwide interdependence and advanced communications technology during the past twenty-five years has made it undeniable that we are one humanity living on one planet together. Yet we are woefully lagging behind in assimilating this knowledge into our actions and institutions, continuing instead to operate from the outdated worldview of national entities, economic growth, and ecological disregard. Globalism, except as conceived for economic gain, is still largely considered a controversial concept.

Nonetheless, truly realizing the entire human population comprises a global family is neither trivial nor a mere sentimentality. In our world today and tomorrow, this realization is a necessity for survival.

How do we recognize family? By blood relationship... commonality of ancestry...shared history. According to the fundaments of biology, we know all the beings on Earth comprise a family; the DNA of all humans is universally the same. Certainly it is time for humanity to acknowledge our family-hood.

One of the primary ways a family creates identity and unity is by sharing the passages of life together—the joys and tragedies, the hopes and disappointments. Families, tribes, and villages the world over, and since the beginning of time, celebrate the birth of their newborn into the world and mourn the death of their loved ones. A sense of family is not created by statistics and intellectual understandings. To bring unity to our global family—our global *village*—we need new ways to feel and express these same fundamental emotions for the members of our family we may never know and yet with whom our lives are inextricably intertwined.

How do we acknowledge the unseen billions who daily affect and contribute to our lives, who have each witnessed the same sun rise today, breathed the same atmosphere, and who each hold their own life as dearly as you hold yours? How do the few who enjoy lifestyles of security and resource consumption justify disregard for the very real hardship which billions of our family endure every day?

How can we comprehend that over 350,000 women will give birth today? How do we welcome the 130 million newborns who arrive in our family each year? How do we share in the hope each one represents and the challenges each will face? How do we pledge ourselves to their nurturance, their protection, and to the world they will inherit?

And too, how do we honor the multitude who died in our family this year? How do we realize our own inescapable mortality in the face of witnessing their passage from life? How do we mourn our inconsolable grief when, via telecommunications, we helplessly witness the brutality, famine, and disease which claim hundreds of thousands of innocent family members?

Finally, how do we responsibly prepare for the realities of a family of nine to eleven billion people in fifty years who will each need a lifetime of food and shelter, meaning and hope?

Our individual and local concerns are so absorbing, most of us simply cannot conceive of the seemingly unrelated lives of six billion others. And if we do, we may feel overwhelmed and powerless. Yet, when we have truly seen ourselves as one ongoing family, how then might we reconceive our world? How might our actions change when we realize our indifference and ignorance today directly affects our family tomorrow?

August 1997

~

ALL THE HUMANS IN THE UNIVERSE

We can say, as we sit in front of the Salt Monument: *This represents all the humans in the manifested Universe.*

Having said that, watch how hard it is for us to accept it!

But why? It would seem patently obvious that the statement is true—in the whole Universe, *human beings* only live on the planet Earth (with the exception of a few who may happen to be in orbit only two hundred miles away). Even if we were (and we haven't yet) to find *intelligent life* (I hate that term, but more about that another time) elsewhere in the galaxy or universe, it could certainly not be definable as *human*. Further, even if we fully subscribe to the idea that a whole host of angelic beings and gods and spiritual individuals who "monitor our progress" and are otherwise engaged in *our* world and even *look* much like humans (as we represent in art, for example)—still, we would have to admit, even they could never actually be called a *human being*.

Human beings are something that happens only here, on Earth. And right now there are six billion individual human beings. No matter where we go in the tens of billions of light years of the Universe, we will not find another *human being*. If we do find extraterrestrial life, it *might* possibly resemble some aspect of Earth life, but whatever it is, guaranteed, it won't be a *human being*. It is just that simple.

So, here we have all the human beings in the universe. Yet we seem to hold a very deep illusion about this. Watch our sense that humans are somehow rained down to Earth from a *magical* universe or heaven. This superstition runs so deep, it is nearly invisible. Where do frogs come from? Or goats? Ants? Trees? We will all answer these questions very simply. Everyone comes from their own kind, from the Earth somehow. Why do we think that *humans*, note it is *only* humans, come from some kind of *divine consciousness* or something?! Watch for this fallacy.

February 2000

~

I Have Died and Been Born So Many Times

I have died—
Alone,
With loved ones,
Painfully after long suffering,
Suddenly from tragic accident,
In peace and safety,
In torment and violence.

I have died so very old.
I have died so very young.
I have died too soon.
I have died by my own choice.

Oh, I have died,
And then died again.
Over 130 million times, I have died
And then died again.

I have died filled with remorse for a life wasted,
And then died fulfilled in a life of love and duty.
I have died in forests, in deserts, in mansions, in gutters,
        in cities, in fields.
I have died with tears, with flowers, with flies, with plastic tubes.
I have died of malaria and diarrhea, of cancers and AIDS,
        of heart disease and calamity.
Oh, I have died,
Again and again.

Oh yes, too, I have been born anew.
Emerging yet again and again
From the womb of a woman.
I have been born
Loved and abandoned, stunted and healthy,
    panicked and peaceful.

I have been born as the answer to a prayer.
I have been born as the curse of a nightmare.
I have been born into poverty, and then into poverty again, and
    yet even again into poverty.
I have sometimes, but more rarely, been born into privilege and
    advantage.
Mostly, I have been born into love and hunger, poverty and
    hardship, disease and familyhood.

Over 320 million times, I have come forth
From the dark, fluid, inner world of a rhythmic heart
To a world which *you* call *the* world.

I have died and been born so many times,
I no longer know a difference between
Joy and grief…A moment or a century…Here or there.
So many times…
And I have only just begun.

April 2000

~

THE *EVERYONE MEDITATIONS* AT THE SALT MONUMENT

It has become a standard segment of every daily session at the Salt Monument. Although its origin was purely organic and quite unintentional, it has yielded unexpected and untold treasures. The idea is simple enough: choose something that *every* single person alive at this moment is doing right now or did at some time during the twenty-four-hour period of a day, and then focus intently on seeing/witnessing as many of the six billion individuals doing that as possible. One particular piece of music has become my framework for this practice. The spirited instrumental piece lasts only three minutes! The objective is to see as many people as clearly as possible in that concentrated timeframe. This occurs in a veritable barrage of images, a torrential montage of split second impressions. Most important is the attempt to include at least one representative of every conceivable sector of humans—spanning all ages, locations, possibilities. The impossibility of this exercise is, of course, inherent: It would mean clearly visualizing over 33 million people each second! However, the mere attempt to do this profoundly expands reality, and yields a remarkably unique glimpse of humanity—a perspective in fact, which we seldom consider or are aware of.

Let us say for example, our focus is on the work humanity has performed during this given twenty-four-hour period of time. We watch all the people involved in the cultivation and preparation of food on the planet—those in the fields and orchards, on foot and in tractors, in the slaughterhouses, in the canning and production factories, on fishing trawlers…We watch the educators, the scientists, the entertainers, the politicians, the inventors. Then there are all the young people whose work is to learn—whether to walk and talk, or read and write, or do their parent's work, or… We watch those whose work is caring for the physical bodies of others—the doctors, surgeons, volunteers, nurses, the veterinarians, the shamans and psychiatrists, the... Then there are those who make our clothes, electronics, equipment, all things in factories, in villages, in assembly lines, sewing, soldering, weaving...There are the miners, the secretaries, the police, the drug lords...Well, you get the picture. But be sure to include those whose work is murder or activism, finance or pornography, ecology or war, journalism or the arts, prostitution or begging...And ad infinitum. Everyone alive on the planet today did *something* as their work.

Just from the *attempt* to truly see humanity as a whole—just the simple facts of existence—we find new insights and perspectives.

We have such a tendency towards distinctions and partialities, it can at first seem difficult to find a focus that truly will include *every*one. The topic for an *everyone meditation* cannot by its very nature exclude an entire segment of humanity. For example, although it is an encompassing focus, we cannot choose *all the children* because this naturally would exclude 4.5 billion people. But we could modify that focus to a viable abstraction that would bring a very unique view of humankind: *all the children that everyone who is alive today either IS or WAS!*

There are endless topics for *Everyone Meditations.* The following are some of the topics I have contemplated during the past year, and a few comments. It should be noted, some of these absolutely include *everyone*, i.e. breathing, heart beating, but others do necessarily exclude a *small* portion of humanity, i.e. there are people without hands, who are blind, and so on. The idea in these cases is to include the exclusions, e.g. being without hands is a way that some people used their hands today; being unable to see with their eyes is the way some people saw today.

Everyone Breathing. This is perhaps the most profound, intense, and accessible *everyone meditation.* Be sure to include those fifteen people breathing their first breath at birth with each of your inhalations and those six people breathing their last breath at death with each of your exhalations. Via the breath, visit with people you know who are far away, or with those you admire and have never met—be aware that they too are breathing now with you, in and out, the same atmosphere. Doing this *everyone meditation* daily will endlessly appreciate in value.

Everyone Speaking/Vocalizing. Listen in on every audible utterance that has taken place among people everywhere on the planet during the past twenty-four hours. But be sure to hear not only all the words in all the languages—also hear the singing, crying, laughing, moaning, gasping, screaming...

Everyone Resting. Journey around the world of people asleep and resting in all the positions and conditions you can imagine. Be sure to range from infancy (or even in the womb) to the elderly, from the healthy to the sick and dying, from comfort/safely to discomfort/danger, and so on.

Everyone's Heart Beating. This one is best if you first have access to an actual preserved human (or other large mammal) heart, so that it can be clearly visualized. Graphic photographs of the heart are also helpful. The idea is not to idealize or romanticize this meditation. We are not talking here about an abstract symbol of love. This meditation is on the actual, physical, constantly throbbing muscle which pulses scores of times every minute of every day, pumping blood throughout the body of every single living person. Be sure to hear the sound of six billion hearts beating within the body of every person, to feel the relentless energy and drive of each heart to continue that beating. See and feel the differences of our newborn/youthful/aging hearts, our diseased hearts, our clogged hearts, our hearts that today will stop.

Everyone Urinating and Defecating. It is an awesome and sobering consideration to sit before the Salt Monument, see what six billion of something looks like, and then try to really comprehend that everyone of those six billion beings excreted something today. No one ever said the *Everyone Meditations* were pretty. In fact, if we are honest and complete in *any* given *Everyone Meditation*, we will encounter all of those things which we consider "bad" and desire to negate/ignore: the gross, the ugly, the painful, the immoral, the cruel, the unjust, and more. But yes—nevertheless, indeed everyone does excrete and during this day, all six billion people found a way and a place to do this. Try taking a journey around the world and really watching this. See what you learn about population concentration and "waste disposal."

Everyone's Hands. The *One Hand* scroll at the Salt Monument is the summary of this meditation: 40,000 years of human hands doing things on this planet. This is an *Everyone Meditation* that can be repeated many, many times and still yield new insights about ourselves. Remember, we use our hands for working, writing, touching, eating, creating, hurting, grooming, and so on. The physical structure of the human hand is considered a major causation of what the human animal has become. Watch what twelve billion hands are doing today.

Everyone at their Work. Another endless exploration worth visiting many times; aforementioned.

What Everyone Saw. "See the whole world in three minutes!" It could be an advertisement to counteract travelmania: "Why limit yourself to what you can see with just one pair of eyes when you can see out of six billion pairs?" But don't censure what is truly seen. Be sure to see not only all the beauty and glory of our planet, all the magnificent life forms and awe-inspiring human creations, but also see the squalor and injustice, the devastation and cruelty, the poverty and human ugliness. See with the eyes of the infant and child, the youths and aged. See all the sights that were seen by humanity during this day.

What Everyone Felt. Delve into all the tides and roller coasters of human emotion. Everyone who is alive today felt *something.* Observe and witness it all—the joy, sorrow, anger, fear, suppression, peace, numbness, hope, grief, frustration, rage, love, and so on. Feel it all.

Everyone in Motion. Even those who are bedridden and paralyzed moved today. (Their caretakers make sure to move their bodies lest they develop sores.) People are in motion in countless ways. Watch six billion people moving around in all climes and cultures: crawling, walking, running, dancing; on animals, in trains, cars, planes, boats, submarines; at work, at play, lovemaking, at prayer…Watch humanity on the move.

Everyone's Face. Whenever I look at the vast, rippled, topmost surface of the Salt Monument, I try to imagine the sea of babies' faces that I am viewing. It devastates me every time: every one of those grains represents a thirteen-to fourteen-month-old… and these are just a *few* of those that age! Every single human face that is or ever has been is unique. Watch six billion unique visages flash by, of every age, of every race, of every person.

Everyone Eating. Of any of the *Everyone Meditations*, this has been perhaps the most unsettling for me. If you were to watch a million locusts obliterate a forest, or a million cattle swallow up a grassland, it would have an impact. But to actually watch six billion people scooping up every possible thing they can find every single day (if possible) to eat from the surface of the Earth is not just sobering but disturbing. Watch as we plunder the oceans' fisheries and ravish the arable soil—displacing, exploiting, or murdering the other living beings on the planet in the process of feeding ourselves. Witness the inequity among humanity—see 500 million ravenous gluttons stuff themselves daily, constantly—consuming and wasting gross quantities of plants and tormented animals, with scarcely a moment of appreciation or awareness, while vast billions of skeleton people wearily scrape dry earth to glean meager morsels. There have been days when even I could not bear to chose this focus for the daily meditation.

There are many more *Everyone Meditations*. They are Endless. Inconceivable. Unattainable... Unforgettable.

March 2000

~

WHATEVER YOU CAN IMAGINE,
SOMEONE IS DOING IT NOW

Just as a note, it is a daily practice during my Salt Monument contemplations: a meditation of images of what these six billion people
are doing right now. Right now. We are all breathing—this of course
is an amazing place to start. Some are sleeping, some are waking,
working, playing, murdering, swimming, making love, teaching,
inventing, healing, destroying, watching television, dying…And
as I have done this each day, I keep expanding. I have come to
believe that: Whatever you can imagine, someone somewhere in
the world is doing it right now.

July 1999

~

So Many

I said a prayer one day
Upon a winded hillside:
"I love you, everyone.
I love you."

Ah, but I had no idea.
No idea.
I forgot to include you and you and you…
How could I have known?
So many.

Now I say a prayer each day,
One day at a time.
It is a prayer to each and every one.
And now I know, as never before:
So many,
We are so many.

There is only one prayer:
For true inner peace.
May each and every one of us know this.

October 1999

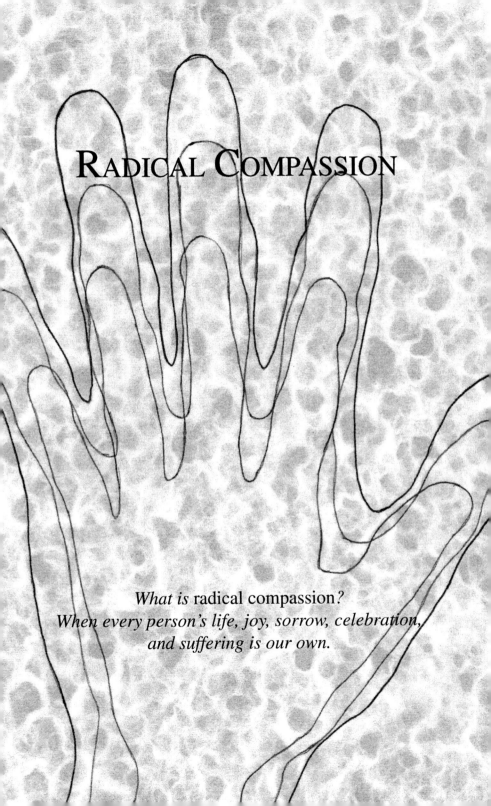

RADICAL COMPASSION

What is radical compassion?
When every person's life, joy, sorrow, celebration,
and suffering is our own.

~

THE ROAD OF RADICAL COMPASSION

When you want to travel the road of radical compassion,
Always start exactly where you are.

Whether you are weary or reverent, overwhelmed, grateful or
pressured, inadequate or alone, or joyous, unfocused, angry, in
love, sick…self-absorbed, humbled…hungry or cold, fortunate,
in fear or disappointed, or…

Wherever you are, *whatever* you are feeling or thinking,
Start *exactly* there.
You do not need to *try* to feel or think anything, nor
Drum up the lofty or abstract
To enter this road.

Begin in the realness of exactly where you are.

Anything will do.
Anything will give you access.
It is itself an infinite road,
So anywhere you start will be the same.

Simply for example:
If you are tired,
Feel your tiredness and let it connect you to the many—so many—
On the road who are also tired.
In your mind's eye,
Go out onto the path of life and seek them out.
Allow yourself to enter into *their* tiredness.
Visit with as many who are also tired on the road as you can—

Of *all* ages, of *all* circumstances, in *all* places.
As much as possible, ignore or forget no one.

Listen to *their* stories,
Feel *their* exhaustion,
Understand *their* reasons.
Be sure to meet with some whose tiredness is *so* great and real
That your own becomes paltry.
Sit a while with these people, and
Let them teach you about tiredness.

They will show you the road of radical compassion.

Always start exactly where you are, and know:
There are as many teachers as there are people
On the road of radical compassion.

February 2000

~

The Prayers Of The World

What if we were to become so acute in our listening as to be able to hear all the prayers being uttered around the world? There are so many prayers every day.

I am not speaking of the noble, high-hearted prayers for lessening the suffering of humankind. I am not speaking of the holy prayers uttered in the churches and temples of worship. No. And neither are these the prayers that theologians discuss, nor those that are considered in the arid heights of philosophical dissertation. They are not even the prayers sincerely defined by genuinely spiritual people in order to elevate the hearts of others.

I am speaking of the simplest prayers, those spontaneously and earnestly expressed in our moments of utter helplessness, in our realization of our powerlessness in the face of life's realities.

It is the prayer of a mother, wishing with all her heart that her child will not die during this night. It is the prayer of the prisoner, yearning for freedom. It is the prayer of celebration for love fulfilled. It is the prayer of the soldier, hoping it is not his best friend who was just killed before his eyes. It is the prayer that there was some way to warm the bitter cold. Or that the merciless heat would abate, or that the rain and flooding would stop, or the life-giving rains would start. It is the prayer for something, *anything*, to eat today. It is the prayer of gratitude for a prayer answered. It is the prayer that one's fatal disease will cease its onslaught. Or that a peaceful death could come quickly. Or that the torturers would simply stop the beating. It is the prayer for one night of safe, peaceful sleep in a city ravaged by violence. It is the prayer of joy for the hope of birth. It is the prayer of a native elder to continue a traditional way of life without being destroyed by modernization. It is the prayer for a job to earn a simple living. It is the prayer of a street child for a few coins. It is the prayer to be saved from a self-destructive addiction. It is the prayer. It is the prayer. It is the prayer.

Oh yes. There are many such prayers, each and every day. Millions upon millions of prayers. Uttered, or perhaps only felt and not even formed into words—but sent out, unheard, from the deepest heart of hearts of single human beings, into the atmosphere of our Earth. Every day. Millions. Even billions. Like an etheric wind circling our planet, the voices, the tears, the pleadings, the hopes—simple heartfelt prayers for the relief of some suffering or difficulty— these transmissions float within the narrow band of our sky just as surely as the radio, television, and satellite transmissions.

We can tune into this station: The Prayers of the World. It is very affecting.

Once heard, these prayers can scarce be forgotten.

March 1998

WHILE I THIS, YOU THAT

While I was dying,
You were being born.

While I was shopping,
You were being tortured.

While I was starving,
You were on vacation.

While I was so cold,
You were so hot.

It is noon here,
While you sleep at midnight.

April 2000

~

The Celery Of Thanksgiving

To me it held a sacredness incomprehensible—the neatly arranged mound of celery at the grand American supermarket was a miracle to behold. *"Look: it's Life! Sprung up from the dust of Earth!"*, I cried out silently to my fellow shoppers, milling about somnambulantly. *"Wake up! Look!"* I laid my hands on the vital stalks as if to receive the blessing of a holy relic.

How can I choose one? Who shall come with me? Which of you is willing to become assimilated into the workings of my body? It seemed an overwhelming decision, and I was aware that my stay at the celery station was unseemly in the context of grocery-store-correctness.

What a strange devolution of hunting and gathering we have come to. No one at the store was even aware that *was* what they were doing: hunting and gathering food—the common denominator of *all* humans and *all* creatures throughout *all* time. Yet here, in this sterile store where *all* food—even the "fresh produce"—is absolutely severed from any indication of having come directly from the Earth, it is easy to forget we are nonetheless creatures roaming around, foraging for survival as we have for scores of millions of years. (Further dissociated still is the rest of the store's food, about 85% of which can more accurately be called "industrial artifacts.")

I laid my hands on the green-hued stalks as in a religious laying on of hands, absorbing the miracle of *that* body...able, willing, to sustain *this* body.

I looked up at the "on sale special" sign above the celery pile. *"Eighteen cents a pound!?"* I called aloud in outrage. *"Eighteen cents!!"* How can this sacred body possibly be valued so cheaply?! How can all of the effort and machinery and labor and transportation and fertilizers (regrettably there was no *organic* celery that day) and merchandizing of this *product* result in a *total* price of just 18 cents a pound?! Further, how can the sacred bodies of those hundred million turkeys be valued at fifty or sixty cents a pound?! If we had to place a value per pound of our children, what would we say? …Thousands of dollars per pound? …Millions? …Priceless? Why do we see their bodies as different from these bodies? Why are the bodies of celery and turkeys simply *products* for sale at a price which clearly shows our disrespect?

I laid my hands on the precious stalks in communion with those who had labored to bring them forth.

There in the store, I stood in a hot, sunny field holding the dirted, weathered hands of a group of *undocumented* people—people who had risked their lives to travel thousands of miles from home, to labor for pennies in the field of the wealthiest nation, to breathe in poisons and bend over for hours, to send a few dollars back to those waiting to dream of a better life, to endure prejudice and injustice. I stood there holding hands with those people, watching how, if those laborers dared enter this store, the upstanding, prim shoppers would shun those very people whose hands had nurtured the foods they were purchasing. How can we not be grateful to, nay even revere, those who have steadfastly done what we would never do in order that we may continue our lifestyle of comfort and ease?

I laid my hands on the priceless stalks in gratitude for all I am blessed with so effortlessly, and with my heart, I finally chose one bunch to take home with me for the sacrament of eating.

I rolled my shopping cart along in that store, aware of the great privilege. I became a person from a land of poverty, famine, war, and despair who had—by some fluke, some merely random chance—been one person from my village who was swooped up by a rescue helicopter and brought to a life of comfort in America. I walked in that store in amazement: rows upon rows of food, such as I had never seen in my entire life! I walked in astonishment: I can buy whatever I want, with no need to hoard it because just as much will be here tomorrow and tomorrow! I tried to contain my elation as I saw by contrast the stressed, emotionless faces of the other shoppers. *Look! Look at this bounty! Look at this blessing!*

It was an ironic advantage though, for always in my mind were the images of my homeland, the faces of my people seared with hunger and hopelessness, and the landscape of devastation. I was trapped inescapably in a dilemma of woe: here *I* am in the store of bounty all the while viscerally knowing the untold misery my family and friends are suffering this minute, every minute, for the rest of their lives. And there is nothing I can do. I think to bring one or two members of my family here, but that itself will take my lifetime. And what of the others? And the others? I suffer the pain of having been *chosen*. Why me? I celebrate and appreciate my great privilege, but I cannot forget the unfairness. I am torn. Irrevocably torn. I know they think of me with gladness for what I have received, but too there is sadness, envy, desolation. I am here in the midst of plenty, yet I cannot forget my family, my homeland. And neither would I forsake this and go back. Torn. I am torn.

It was all I could do to complete my shopping, wandering through those aisles, shedding only a few tears there in the store. Later that night, at home, alone...I wept.

November, 1999

$\sim$

Who Among Us?

How many are making decisions for all of us?

     A handful.

How many are living the consequences of those decisions?

     Six billion.

What happens if we ask each of the six billion people to help decide:

Do you want war where you live?
Do you want to see your children die
     from malnutrition and disease caused by poverty?
Do you want your homeland plundered
     for the profit and convenience of others you do not know?
Do you want to slave in a factory, beg for food,
     sell yourself or your children, or live in the street?
Do you want to live daily in terror of cruelty, oppression,
     violence, or tyranny?

Who among us, who among six billion, will say yes to these questions for themselves and their loved ones?

     Not one!

Then why are a handful of people daily making decisions that directly and indirectly cause all this to happen, not to just one or a handful but to billions? Billions of us!

What if each and every person in the world helped decide?

Impractical?! Radical democracy?! Impossible?! Yes, perhaps. Things are far too complex for such a thing to work. But shouldn't the handful of people involved in decisions consider this?

Shouldn't we all?

February 1998

~

A Knock At The Door

In morning prayers today, I found myself focused on the legacy of past suffering around the globe inflicted by humans upon one another. As I journeyed to each area on our Earth, I felt the tragedy of those events: the destruction of cultures, the devastation of peoples, the brutality of wars, the wantonness of domination. When I faced to the East, after I passed through the enslavement of Africans and the decimation of the native people on this continent and crossed the Atlantic, I entered Europe. There I was overcome with a vivid, palpable experience of what we now call the Holocaust. I was the children hiding in the filth of the latrines of a concentration camp; I was the dignified, educated professionals of Poland who had my home, my wealth, my treasures stripped from me; I was the frightened people squashed standing for hours in the railroad car wondering what fearsome destination we were being taken to; I was the miserable prisoners shoveling multitudes of skeletons of my relatives into enormous pits; I was the walking dead scraping a simple pictogram of a butterfly, our symbol of hope in a world of horror, into the cramped wooden slab I called my bed; I was the innocent families huddled behind the walls and under the floors listening to the dreaded Gestapo's soldiers, who came in the middle of the night and murdered or captured our friends and neighbors. I was so overwhelmed in the suffering, I fell to the floor, and wept and wept.

The horror, the suffering, the cruelty that has occurred throughout history and in every land… it is utterly and incomprehensibly huge, and we, the human race, may never be able to fully redeem ourselves from the ugly energy with which our world has been so deeply stained. How can we heal these wounds we have bled and burned and buried into our Earth and into the cells of our children and our children's children? How can we reclaim our dignity when the anguished screams of our ancestors still reverberate on our lands and in our hearts? What ceremonies of purification and obeisance can we offer to cleanse ourselves of the legacy of human cruelty?

As a living being, I am the cellular location of all this. I am the history of our earth's birth, and that of our solar system and even our universe, my cells containing the explosions and cataclysms, the expansions and vastness of billions of years. I am the history of life on earth, my cells containing the billions of years of forms and development. I am the history of my species, the humans. Some people believe in past lives, specific personal lives they can identify with. But within each of us is the past (and present) life of every human, as well as every life form, and every element (certainly within our galaxy). Every life, every feeling, every thought, every experience exists within us, hanging in potentiality for our awareness.

As such, I stand as a representative of my human family and, before the universe and our Earth, I ask forgiveness. Please forgive what I, the human being, have done. Please heal these wounds I have inflicted upon myself, the human body. Ah! Let us pray and forgive.

June 1997

~

To The Heroic and Unheralded

Let us sing in praise of you,
The many, so many:
Unheralded, unacknowledged,
Unknown, unacclaimed.

You, who tried to be kind.
You, who survived untold challenge.
You, who loved your children.
You, who did your best.
You, who was faithful.
You, who helped others.
You, and you, and you…

Each of you,
Heroic champions of an uncharted life of rigor.
We hail your valiant journey.

October 1999

~

Grieving With The Grieved

Flower arranging, and in tears, on my knees: swept away in the beauty and poignancy. I am always aware: "no one dies without flowers from now on." I saw photos in the news of people grieving the death of their loved ones—the bereaved of seventeen men who were killed in the explosion on the US destroyer, *Cole*, off the coast of Yemen.

But why *these* seventeen only and this day? Why do we *want* to see photos of *their* loved ones' grief, but *only* these: Americans who died in military duty, stimulating patriotic outrage? Why?! Why cry only for *some*? We have not seen photos of the recently murdered Palestinian's bereaved. Or the impoverished thousands of children who die each day. Or... or... or...

The Salt Monument is the only answer for me. We must cry *each* day, for each one—in our hearts—otherwise, it doesn't make sense. We must be outraged and heartbroken with each and *every* violent act. We must acknowledge our complicity and indifference in *every* indignity and deprivation.

At today's global roll call time, I happened to be standing at the Salt Monument. Raising my hand with millions, nay billions, I saluted us. Oh yes. All that the Salt Monument is and can be, we need *so* deeply.

October 2000

~

Witnesses To Suffering

We can no longer deny that we are witnesses to an enormity of suffering. There was a time on this planet when the only suffering we were aware of was that in our own local vicinity, and it is true, this was (and still is) almost always enough in itself to be fertile ground for compassion and action. In those times, the various miseries of others across the globe were entirely or largely unknown to one another.

This is no longer the case. With the globalism of communication, we are privy to the travails of any group of people, creatures, plant life, even "ecosystems," on our planet. There is always that question of *involvement*.

For example, during the recent summer incursion of moths, when 600 moths are writhing in agony and I am there as a witness, how much do I allow myself to become *involved* in their torment? Do I let myself feel it? If they were in another room, or another country, does that lessen their agony? Why should it lessen mine? Or let us bring the example more pointedly: If I were to travel today to any one of the thousands of refugee camps in Africa to help an effort to provide food to a vast, seemingly endless crowd of impoverished, undernourished people, including thousands of pathetically thin, orphaned, and weak young children, I am sure after my first several hours I would be utterly devastated with grief and a sense of hopelessness. Why? Because I would *feel* for them and their situation. But if I see that scene in a television documentary, why should I feel it less? Simply because I am not physically *there*? What does that matter? And even if I am not there, and I don't happen to see it on television, but I know that it is happening nevertheless, is not that same *feeling* in me?

Thomas Merton brilliantly titled one of his books *Conjectures of a Guilty Bystander.* He had realized it. We are guilty, simply because we are here and standing by, that is, witnessing, the atrocities.

It is a great challenge in life, to be able to hold all the dimensions of our world/reality/spirituality simultaneously, fully, and with true feeling. It is in many of my thoughts. The challenge is—how can we reconcile: our awareness and feeling of the suffering of all others, with our personal comforts and securities, with our spiritual bliss and knowledge? This is the work of the *bodhisattvas*, who live in the world that *all* may be released from suffering and know fulfillment.

June 1998

~

Unfair, Unjust

Unfair.
Unjust.
Inequitable.

These are the truths.

Oh, we tell ourselves so many stories
To explain this away,
To excuse our complicity,
To mask this grave ill.

Any explanation will do:
Religious—Oh, many lifetimes…you did this before…
       so you are born into this travail…
Political—Oh, this country has this history…
       so these people have this…
Economic—Oh, this poverty was caused…
       you have this debt…developing nation…

We all know, we all know:

No *one* person truly has more of the right
To eat or grow or live or be safe
Than any *other* person.

We all, each and every one,
Have, expect, deserve
The same right
To have, to live, to thrive.

We just don't know how to get this to happen now
And so,
We pretend,
We tell stories,
We become righteous.

But deep within
We all know:

Unfair.
Unjust.
Inequitable.

October 2000

~

PRIVILEGE...THE BURDEN OF MY HYPOCRISY

For the arrogant,
Privilege is a license for disdain, superiority, and callousness.

For the thoughtful, privilege is an enormous debt and even shameful.
To receive so much when one has done nothing to deserve it
Leaves one feeling both blessed and inadequate.

I am no better than you.
Yet I have food enough to become overweight,
While you daily struggle for a single morsel to eat.
I have done nothing to deserve this warmth
During the cold winter,
While you endure the frigid reality each day.
I did nothing to earn the comfort and luxury of this home,
Which you would gladly share with one hundred of your people.
My health, my good fortune, my opportunities,
        my leisure, my conveniences—
These all simply happened to me as little by my own doing as
Your suffering, your disadvantage,
        your daily struggle, your oppression
All simply happened to you.

I have nothing to be proud of.
I did nothing to earn my privilege.
It is an infinite debt of gratitude, compassion, and shame.
You have nothing to be ashamed of.
You did nothing to earn your disadvantage.
It is your nobility to bear it.

I do not know how to extend my cloak of privilege
            onto your disadvantage.
Instead, it is a mantle of stigma I wear each day.
I try my best not to abuse my privilege,
But instead I am imbedded in continual hypocrisy.

I try my best not to take on additional privileges.

The burden of my hypocrisy is already
More painful than I can bear.

February 1999

Songs
At
The Salt Monument

There is a song every day at the Salt Monument…
With so many people,
there is always *a song to be sung.*

~

The Songs At The Salt Monument

There is a song every day at the daily Salt Monument observance accompanied by Sonata, the harp. These songs are purely spontaneous and mysteriously inspired. As I begin each time, I have no idea what will be sung. Some songs are to the dying, or those being born; some are to the survivors of a natural calamity (recently floods in China, Hurricane Mitch in Central America). Sometimes a song is for one specific person somewhere in the world—a mother who painfully placed her newborn infant where hopefully a more fortunate person might find the baby and provide a better life for the child; an elder aborigine watching his nation destroyed by invaders; an isolated prisoner who has lost hope after so many years. There are nearly six billion people, each with a life, with a face and a name, with dreams, with suffering, with hope. There is always a song to be sung.

During this past week, I recall there was a song to the children of the world who are homeless, parentless, and destitute living in the streets of cities, where they beg, steal, prostitute themselves and drug themselves with glue to escape their enormous pain. Not all songs are so sad. Today's song was a quiet celebration of the countless millions of unsung heroes who, in the autumn of their life, reflect upon their brief journey knowing they have been truly kind and good, having done the best they can in all ways, living a life of simple anonymity, loved by a mere handful of people who have known them.

Sometimes the songs are sung in the first person—that is, I become a person singing their life song. Other times it is *my* person singing of someone. Always the songs are heartfelt and poignant. Usually the song is finished simply because my tears have drenched me and I simply can no longer breathe.

These songs are always sung in languages I do not know (and do not exist in any lexicon), but which I always understand. Because I am not encumbered by thinking processes to arrive at specific wording, each song flows straight from feeling into sound. Simultaneously as I feel it and hear it, I understand its meaning. In the intensity of the moment, enclosed in the harp's cocoon of sacred music, expressed in the exotic tones of an unknown language, these Salt Monument songs are daily and profoundly heart-rending when they come through. I am well aware that afterward, in the unfeeling, frozen black-and-whiteness of writing and English, they may seem simplistic and even perhaps foolish. Nevertheless, it has occurred to me that perhaps these should be preserved.

A few weeks ago, after a particularly unusual (and distracting) spate of social activities, the memorable song, "Forgive Me, I Have Forgotten You," was sung. I sat down for the daily observance, and saw how, in my superficial self-absorption, I had completely forgotten nearly every one of the six billion others in the world. It speaks from the viewpoint of truly recognizing our family is the whole human family. Imagine if a member of your immediate family was suffering a terrible calamity, and you knew of it, but then your own personal involvements so eclipsed your senses, that you actually and completely forgot what was happening to your own child, your father or mother, your brother or sister, your grandparents. When you did finally remember and you came back to be with them, in regret and humility you would admit your forgetting and sadly ask their forgiveness.

This is what *is* happening on the planet. We have completely forgotten one another.

The impact of this song was so profound, I wrote the translation down.

November 1998

~

Forgive Me, I Have Forgotten You

I have forgotten you,
My child starving here in my arms.
I have forgotten you,
My father dying alone in the street.
Forgive me, for I have forgotten you,
My mother, beaten and raped in the bitter cold.
Forgive me, I have forgotten you,
My brother imprisoned for declaring the rights of our people.

Forgive me for I have forgotten you
While I was so immersed in my comforts and desires,
My petty concerns and trivial inconveniences,
My vain entertainments and empty distractions.

Engulfed in vanity, ego gratifications and self-absorption,
I forgot you even exist,
My own family.
I have forgotten you—
Each of you.
Lost in my personal melodrama,
I have forgotten you exist.
I have failed to comfort you.
I have left you alone and neglected.
Forgive me.

You have lived in a nightmare,
You have nobly endured untold hardship,
While, unfeeling, I left you to suffer.
I did not come forward on your behalf.

Forgive me.
I have said I love you in my heart.
I intended to honor you, to protect you, to care for you.
But in truth, I have forgotten you.

Please, forgive me.

I meant to help you, but I have done nothing.
Even worse, to avoid my guilt in this,
I have forgotten you.

Forgive me.

November 1998

~

WINTER SONG

Light the candles on this day,
Celebrate the light.
Celebrate the love you share.
Rejoice together.
All around the northern cold,
Candles lit in hope.

Treasure one another.
Cherish one another.
For our time together is so short.

Honor one another.
Love one another.
Our time here is precious.

Gone so soon.

December 1998

~

THE REFUGEES' SONG

TO ALL REFUGEES, INSPIRED BY THE KOSOVAR EXODUS

Take these few things we own
And let us go
On a road to somewhere.
Somewhere else.

Leave behind this place we know as home.
Leave behind our lives, our memories,
For we must go.
We must go somewhere else.

Here we have known the sun rise and set countless times.
Here our children were born.
Here our parents died.
Here we have strained our backs and arms
To carve out our meager needs.
Here, our home.

We leave only because we must.

What is it you could possibly want here?
You, who have invaded our homes
With violence and hatred
So cruel and close
That we can only choose to leave?

Take care of this place if you would, at least,
While we are gone on this dusty road
To somewhere else.

In my heart, I only hope:
One day I will return
Home.

May 1999

~

THE CHINA DOLL

Sometimes harp songs at the Salt Monument emerge similarly to a *Syzygy* painting: a fragment of feeling or image is vaguely perceived, gradually becoming clearer, than another piece and another are added, all the while I have no idea what I am witnessing. The song and its meaning are revealed as I simultaneously *become* the seeing and feeling voice of an unknown person in their particular place and moment. This song was particularly striking in this way. It began with the image of a face; I then realized it was actually the face of a beautiful, precious china doll. The images unfolded as the song progressed—a doll, a mother, a child...a *dead* child...a burial...a simple, heart-wrenching question. By the time the grief-filled dilemma of the scene and song had emerged in my awareness and fully become my own, I could no longer sing it, I was weeping so.

Oh sweetheart,
Your face so still and beautiful
Just like a china doll...
Your china doll.

You have always had this doll with you,
Wherever you went,
Wherever.
But now...

Do you need your doll now, sweetheart,
Where you have gone this time?

I could lay her here beside you
To be buried forever with you
In this dark silence.

But now, it is *me*,
Not *you*,
Who cannot part with her.
Tell me, sweetheart,
Do you need her now
As much as I do?

Tell me.

October 2000

~

Come My Brothers and Sisters—
For Sarvodaya Shramadana

Dr. A. T. Ariyaratne is the founder and president of Sarvodaya Shramadana which is active throughout Sri Lanka. In Sanskrit, the first word means "the awakening of all" and the second, "shared giving and work," which is the basis of this grass roots, humanitarian, peace-building organization. People who have been in centuries of gruesome conflict with one another come together to rebuild their communities in harmony, sometimes from the literal ruins of their own civil warfare. The following song appeared at the Salt Monument one morning, in honor of their work.

Come my brothers and sisters,
Let us rebuild our village together
Out of the rubble of our hatred,
United finally in our grief and devastation.

Come my brothers and sisters,
Let us adopt these children
Who we have left orphaned
In the wake of our rage and violence.
Finally reminded, unforgettably now,
Of love and tolerance.

Come my brothers and sisters,
Let us till our soils together
With the tools that were our killing tools,
Listening at last to one another
To grow, rather than destroy.

May 1999

~

Our Dignity—Lost

We were once a proud people,
Standing tall in dignity.
We knew every plant and creature.
We cared for the place of our ancestors.
We understood how to provide for ourselves and our children.

Now we are here
At this place of desolation
Far from our homeland,
Driven away by drought, famine, and war.
Now we have nothing.
Even our dignity is lost.

Look at us now.
Crumpled and disgraced.
Stunned and listless.
Waiting to be fed.

The older ones die quickly.
Our young children do too.
The rest of us are
Waiting…

November 1999

≈

To Those Who Are Achingly Alone Today

I was heartlessly abandoned at birth.
I was orphaned and am now lost.
I am here dying alone.
I am choosing to end my life.
I am so alone.

To each of you feeling so alone today,
Even amidst the billions of your sisters and brothers,
I hope somehow in your terrible aloneness and implacable sadness
You might feel this simple thought of tenderness.

Because I *am* thinking of you,
Right now, today.
I flow with tears for you,
Now, today.

To you, abandoned at birth, I hold you close with love.
To you, orphaned and lost, I share kindness.
To you, dying alone, I honor your life's journey.
To you, choosing to end your life, I feel for your despair.

Achingly alone as you may be,
My thoughts are with you.

July 1999

~

"CAN YOU HEAR ME?"

I came to the Salt Monument today, tired and empty, overwhelmed as I am every day that there really are so many people. What can I sing? What can I offer in prayer? How can I serve my family here in this ceremony today? I sat down to begin my session, sitting first in meditation and then bringing forward Sonata (the harp) to sing. What can be sung? I do not know where or how.

The harp began with a few high, solitary notes in a plaintive, simple melody. And then a voice—a tiny, shaky voice came forward. "Can you hear me? Can anyone hear me?" It was the heart of a young child crying for help, crying for listening, just barely audible. The plea was so innocent, so sincere, so desperate for some hope—I choked in tears. To me, it was a child in the middle of the night somewhere in Asia, praying for hope. "Can anyone hear me?" One child…one person in the midst of six billion.

Finally, recovering myself, I sang directly into the heart of Sonata: "I hear you. I *do* hear you." What could I say? I can do nothing. I can help in no way. I knew my contact with that child was more ephemeral than a drop of dew, more evanescent and imaginary than a fleeting dream. "I do hear you, dear one," I cried out my futile message with all my love and strength.

It was one of the smallest, most heart-wrenching moments I have felt at the Salt Monument. There is a poignant miracle in one person listening to and loving another—one person to one person. Sometimes, just knowing we have been heard can help. Perhaps in the darkness of that night, a child somehow felt heard.

September 1999

～

Can We Laugh In The Face Of Death?

This song erupted a cappella at the Salt Monument as a declaration of the solidarity and invincibility of a people burdened with untold suffering and yet strong in resolve.

Can we laugh in the face of death,
Even with tears in our eyes?

Can we celebrate the blessing of life
Even in the midst of humiliation and starvation?

Oh, this is our greatest strength,
The greatest wisdom.
This is the true Power of the Human Spirit:

To sing, even in the darkest hour.
To forge ahead with dignity and joy.
To fully feel our individual woes
And know beyond them.

November 1999

~

If You Knew I Thought Of You

If you knew I thought of you all day, and
Wept a puddle for you, and
Cried out in the injustice and cruelty that you have been dealt,

Would it help?

Would it ease the pain,
Bring you hope,
Warm your heart?

Would it make any difference?

To Rodolfo Montiel Flores, in Mexico, of whom I heard this morning: imprisoned for his activism to stop the deforestation of his homeland; tortured, and now suffering serious illness associated with that torture, specifically of his testicles. Others have already been killed. My anguish for him seemed so futile; my devotion at the Salt Monument to each individual in suffering seemed so delusional; and yet too, I realized, if he *did* know I had thought of and cried for him throughout my day, it probably would make some small difference to him.

Postscript: Rodolfo Montiel Flores was released in November, 2001, following an international campaign on his behalf.

December 1999

~

A Few Songs and Notes

When our saltwater tears fall into the salt water of the deaths at the Salt Monument—what does this mean? It is a *very* beautiful thing. It is *all* as the sea: our tears, the water of our bodies, the water of the Earth—all joined together.

~ ~ ~

I became a song of a person who had worked for many years around the world with the organization known as Doctors Without Borders. It was an amazing testimony to what they had seen. My notes are far too scanty to give substance to the experience of this person which affected me so profoundly that morning. "I have seen the children…" (followed with heartful descriptions of their suffering from malnutrition, diseases, traumatic exposure to heinous violence, orphaned…) "I have seen the elders…" (similarly descriptions of their suffering, pain, isolation, loss of home/culture…) "I have seen the wounded…" (those hurt in violent conflicts…), and so on. "We must stop hurting one another. Please. Can we? Can we stop?"

~ ~ ~

A beautiful song appeared at the Salt Monument, called The Wind. Sung by a native person about the wind in their homeland, first describing how the wind blew the fragrance of luscious flowers and foliage; then how the wind witnessed horrors, atrocities, and destruction; and finally asking the wind to blow away the sounds, sights, and memories of those horrors.

~ ~ ~

At my morning prayers, I fell deeply in tears and wrote these notes:
I seek to bring the Salt Monument to the world, not because I want
to or it is convenient, nor for glory or honor. I do it—as those who
carried the Ark of the Covenant, tenting it in the desert and conse-
crating it in a great temple—out of a sense of duty, out of love and
hope for all people. It would be far easier and more preferred by
me to retreat with the Salt Monument now. I would choose this for
myself. But it is my duty to do this—I am supposed to bring the
Salt Monument to the people.

~ ~ ~

I became the anguish of a boy, about six or seven years old, whose
mother had just died, leaving him alone in the world. I so much
became him, I saw the grave, saw the dirt being flung into it, felt
myself as him wanting to throw himself into the grave. I was truly
overcome with his grief.

March 1999

~

I Did Not Lie Dying...

I found a worm
Parched on the scorching driveway of the morning sun today.

I did not lie dying in the sun today...
Yet I am that thirst.

I did not hold my starving child in my arms today...
Yet I am that grief.

I did not hear my mother beaten and raped today...
Yet I am that horror.

I was not there when my brother was shot dead in the war today...
Yet I am that loss.

I did not stand helpless as my father was tortured for his beliefs today...
Yet I am that torment.

I did not sit, orphaned, with my sister in the gutter today...
Yet I am that despair.

The forest of my ancestors was not forever destroyed today...
Yet I am that devastation.

I was not released from a life of misery in a squalid slaughterhouse today...
Yet I am that suffering.

I did not stand in joy beside my beloved at our wedding today…
Yet I am that celebration.

I did not gaze into the newborn eyes of my great-grandchild today…
Yet I am that hope.

I did not blossom into a flower in the field today…
Yet I am that purity.

August 1997

~

Oh, Flowers!

Oh flowers, most beautiful.
I live to gaze at these flowers today.

Thousands upon thousands
Of exquisite tulips.
Brilliant, fragrant, remarkable.
People scarcely glance.

But I look at them
Having been locked up in a dark prison for years,
Finally released to a day of sunlight and vision.

Oh, *you* would gaze upon them with loving tears too—
Just to see *one*!

But instead, you see
So many.
It is always hard for us to deeply appreciate that which is
Common, plentiful, numerous.

April 2000

Go Forth With Dignity

Go forth with dignity—
Whatever fate may befall you.

For those in prison, on death row,
On streets as beggars…
For those defeated, marginalized, brutalized…
For the majority of humanity…
For the utter "nobodies"…
To us all:

Go forth with dignity,
Always,
Whatever the circumstances.

To hold yourself with the highest honor,
Embodying the greatest virtues of being human—
However lowly others may be in their treatment of you,

Go forth with dignity—
Whatever fate may befall you.

December 2000

Our Children

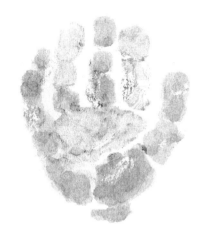

Every one of us was once a child.

~

THE WORLD OF THE UNBORN

On any given day, there are about 100 million people swimming, floating, nearly weightless, inside the watery darkness of another human being. The only world these people live and grow in for nine uninterrupted months is very different than the world they and we are born into. "I come forth from the dark, fluid, inner world of a rhythmic heart, to a world which *you* call *the* world." Let us visit the world of the floating people—the unborn.

~ *Warm.* Ah…such a deliciously perfect warmth. Always. The climate here is always very warm, varying only a few degrees.

~ *Dark.* There is only darkness here. Sometimes there is an extremely faint red glowing-ness but only very rarely.

~ *Rhythmic.* A constant, ceaseless rhythmic pulse is audible and always heard. It never stops. Sometimes it is faster, sometimes it is slower, but always it is there. A muffled and distinct: Thump, thump, thump, thump.

~ *Self-Fulfilling.* Everything that is needed is right here; everything is taken care of without effort. Desire and fulfillment are utterly unified; nourishment, elimination, oxygen, fluids—all occurs seamlessly.

~ *Non-Dualistic.* There is an absence of all dualistic conception. Everything that is, simply is. There is nothing else but is-ness.

~ *Utterly Different Than* Your *World.* It is different in almost endless ways from *your* world. There is no time, no expectation, no self, full consciousness with no distinctions.

Everyone one of us has lived in that same world. Although significant differences between us happen there—the neuro-chemistry, genetics, nutrition, and psychological make-up of both the mother and the fetus have an intrinsically immediate and lifelong impact—nevertheless, we all know the dark, floating experience within our deepest cellular being.

Ultimately, this is a sublime meditation practice: to return to the womb self. If we read about any style of meditation with this in mind, we will see that the instructions are basically describing the womb experience. But it is so much easier to simply allow ourselves to return to that state of being by vividly recalling it. It is universally accessible.

April 2000

~

Birth Is A Kind Of Death

What we call "birth" is actually a kind of death. Leaving the womb world to enter the world we call *the world* effects a transition of the magnitude and profundity of death. For instance, birth marks the *end*: of oneness and non-differentiation, of weightlessness and near-perfect temperature, of all-needs-met-nourishment, of non-duality, of no-thinking, of no ego-self...It is also the *beginning* of: time, duality, thought, ego, light, sight, interaction, desire, and...(Oh yes, it is also the beginning of the world of broken dreams, but that is another topic.)

Wordsworth said, "Our birth is but a sleep and a forgetting..."

Yes, but even further. What if birth is just another kind of death? If we go into the experience of the womb and truly *be* there, and from there feel the call gradually arising that we will (and must) depart from our (womb) world—if we really go into this and feel it, it feels very similar to death. We are faced with a *forced* transition from what is familiar to what is utterly unknown. Look at how absolutely unimaginable the world we are born into is from the world in which we lived during our nine womb-months. There is no way to prepare, expect, comprehend the world we are born into. It is SO different. Death is no different. Birth and death are both merely transitions—*forced* transitions along an otherwise unknown continuum. There is much to think on this.

November 2000

~

Everyone Was Once An Infant

Everyone of us was once an infant…dependent, helpless…
Everyone of us was once a child…innocent, hopeful.
We send a blessing of love to each of you
     who are children today—
That you may be cared for, loved, nourished,
     protected, and educated.

February 1999

~

Pledge To The Newborn

Today, as I held the birth cup—holding one grain of salt for each of
       those born today—to my heart,
I pledged myself as a parent does, with selfless devotion.
What if, as a world family, we pledged ourselves
To every one of our newborn children?

If you are hungry, I will feed you.
If you are cold, I will warm you.
If you are frightened, I will comfort you.
If you are sick, I will care for you.
If you are lost, I will guide you.
If you are happy, I will delight with you.
If you are victorious, I will celebrate with you.
If you have something to say, I will listen.
If you call, I will answer.

January 2000

~

I HAVE SEEN CHILDREN...

I have seen children who have been brutally beaten.
I have seen children who were raped.
I have seen children chained to rug looms.
I have seen children missing arms and legs.
I have seen children turned into fierce soldiers.
I have seen children forced to shoot their own parents.
I have seen children sold into slavery and prostitution.
I have seen children who have witnessed untold horror and cruelty.
I have seen all this *every day*.
Every day I have seen 20,000 to 30,000 children die from
malnutrition and poverty.
Every day I have seen millions upon millions of children living in
wretched refugee camps.

I have seen these children carry these wounds every day for the
rest of their lives.

What can we be thinking?

August 1999

~

To Those Who Were Born Today

Oh, embodied miracle of birth—
Newborn human!
You are evidence of the greatest of mysteries.

Welcome to our world.
You are our hope, our future.

We cherish and praise your purity and innocence.
You are our teacher
Of wordless love and wisdom,
Of vulnerability and dependence,
Of unfettered trust.

Wherever and whoever you are,
Your urge to laugh and play
At *every* opportunity, in *any* situation,
Will be a constant reminder of the true joy of life.
We will treasure your smiles and laughter.

I wish I could say:

You will have a life
Of security, peace, opportunity,
Freedom, health, and dignity.

I wish I could tell this to each of you born today and know it to be true.
But it is not.

What I know is:
Of each ten of all of you born today one or two will
        die before your fifth birthday.
Nearly every one of you has been born into
        perilous conditions of poverty.
Many of you will witness grievous horrors and atrocities
        during your childhood.
Few of you will overcome the hardship, tyranny, disease, and
        suffering of your homeland.
Even fewer of you will know the security and comfort
        which is commonplace to me, and
Of which you will futilely fantasize when you become older.

I wish I could say:

You have been born into a world of
Magic, mystery, beauty, love,
Abundance, peace, and bliss.
I wish I could tell you each this because I do know it to be true.
But I also know:
It is not likely this is the world you will discover during your life.

I welcome you to our world with all my heart,
And truly wish each of you the best in life.

December 1997

~

THE STADIUM OF DEATH

I may perhaps be accused of being not only lurid but irreverent as well. But it is an image that is useful in really comprehending a tragic reality, and could even be extended (both playfully and metaphorically) quite further than I will choose to take it here. It is a very interesting representational model: the Stadium of Death.

Every day, somewhere between 20,000 to 33,000 children under the age of five die from causes directly related to poverty. I consciously enact this at the Salt Monument every day. Every day. Every day. It doesn't stop. What do these many unfortunate, neglected infants and children look like?

Let us imagine a sports stadium. Most hold about 40,000 to 60,000 people. There actually are a few huge stadiums that do have 150,000 capacity, which would thus hold all the people who die around the world in a single day. Let us use a mid-size stadium familiar in this locale—Mile High Stadium in Denver has a capacity of (precisely) 76,273. In two *sell-out* sessions each and every day, we could in our imaginations, seat all the people who die in the world every day. Let's say this is where they come after they have said goodbye to their loved ones and before they are finally dead. *"Children under five, over here. Your seats are over here. All impoverished children under five, enter through doors A through M. A through M here."*

Let us witness a stadium fully half-filled with these young children. Every day. Every day.

It is so unconscionable that this is actually happening in our world today and every day. Once you have vividly imagined this, I promise: it is an image you will never forget.

What announcement shall we make to these children via the public address system of that stadium as they sit, waiting for the end of the *game*. What would you say?

July 1999

~

SONG OF THE UNFORTUNATE CHILDREN

I sit at the Salt Monument and hear
The voices of children around the world—
The children whose life facts can only be called
Unfortunate.

"My parents were beaten and killed.
"My arms were deformed at birth from poisons we are living in.
"My grandfather's forest was destroyed and
       we were sent to this dry place.
"My whole village is starving.
"My parents died of AIDS and only I am left
       to care for my brothers and sisters.
"I saw my parents cut to pieces.
"I haven't eaten for a week; my grandmother gives me all she can.
"On our street, the gunmen shoot at anyone.

"I do not understand.
Can you help me understand:
Why is it like this for me?

"I have heard of places where children eat every day several times,
Where they play and go to school all day.
I have heard there are children who have never wondered

If they will starve this winter,
Or if someone will kill a member of their family today,
Or if they can bear to walk the two hundred miles away from home
       to stay in a tent city with 100,000 others
Just to be safe from death and destruction.

"I do not understand.
Can you tell me:
Why can't it be like that for me?"

October 1999

~

Song Of The Child-Rug-Weaver

Thread by thread,
Thread by thread,
Hour by hour,
Day by day,
Rug by rug,
Year by year.

I can still remember my home,
And my mama and papa.
They said I needed to work
So they could feed my brothers.
I was five years old
When they brought me here and said,
Goodbye.

Chained to this loom,
Here I work,
Thread by thread,
Thread by thread,
Hour by hour,
Day by day,
Rug by rug,
Year by year.
Weaving the ancient patterns.

My friend next to me
Has been here
Seven years longer than me.

When will you be done? I ask.

I know not, I know not.

Thread by thread,
Day by day,
Year by year.

June 2000

~

To Three Born This Day

On this day, as you are born, your life stretches out before you—to unfold unknown to you and all those around you. We only know the future by going into that present which awaits us. Here, to three children born somewhere on this planet this day among some 364,320 others, the unknown future of your life is revealed.

Ashti, the sickly girl child born in a small village in India. No one knows it today, but someday you will rise from these humble beginnings to become a leader of your people, a modest and celebrated bringer of freedom and dignity to an impoverished, forsaken place. Many blessings to you in fulfilling your destiny.

Kahlib, the boy today born in Burma to his loving parents, the fifth child in a hardworking family. You will grow to work in the rice fields, to marry and bring forth three children. In your life you will labor hard, have little, believe in goodness, and die after 64 years.

Melar, the boy born in Syria. Your parents proudly celebrate your healthy birth and your place as first male child in their family. Their hopes and dreams lie with you. Yet you will be killed as a soldier in your 19th year.

What if we knew the stories of our lives, or the lives of those we love, before they unfolded? How different life would seem.

January 1999

~

OH MAMA...

"Oh Mama, I am so cold."

"I am so hungry."

"I feel so sick."

"Oh Mama, I think today is my day to die."

"Why can't we go back to our home?"

"I am so afraid of those men with guns."

"Mama, I saw something horrible."

"Why must I leave you?"

"Mama, something terrible happened to my brother."

"Mama, Mama,
Where are you?"

October 1999

SAYING GOODBYE

*Let us stand together in
awe of the great mystery of death,
which we each face.*

~

United By Grief

One day, at the honoring of the world's deaths of that day, the image of an African woman came forward. She slowly reached into the death cup with the salt, carefully took out one grain, and sadly dropped it into the water herself. She said simply, "My daughter died today." An Arab man followed and did the same, saying, "It was my son who died today." Next, another, "My father." And another, "My wife," and another and another and another…

A twenty-five mile long queue trailed outside, as 150,000 loved ones of those who had died each came to the Salt Monument to claim their loss. We grieved together, weeping from the heart.

Isn't this enough to bring us together?

It is a sad observation perhaps, but there is nothing which unites us more genuinely and enduringly than great grief. Danger and adversity can unite us, but only temporarily. Celebration and music unite us as well, but again, the effects are usually short-lived. We can even see the most affecting unity occurs at the juncture of a funeral, which combines celebration, music, and grief all in one occasion.

When a catastrophic event occurs, or a shocking tragedy comes close to home, people are stricken with a sense of compassion and realization. But we do not need to wait for a devastating occurrence to be reminded that life is precious and we are each vulnerable.

There is always enough grief on the planet to unite us.

February 2000

~

I THOUGHT THERE WOULD BE ANOTHER DAY
SONG OF A MOTHER, DYING OF AIDS, TO HER YOUNG CHILD

I thought there would be
Another day to hear your laughter.
Another day to look into your eyes.

I hoped there would be
Another year to see you grow.
Another year to watch your dreams come true.

Ah…
I do not mind dying here today.
To leave this vale of pain and anguish,
This, I do not mind.

But oh…my dear one.
I cannot bear it that
I leave you here…alone…
Oh god.

September 2000

~

To Those Who Died Today

A few of us passed through that portal we call death today.
Seen among the multitude of us all,
It seems only a few.
Yet we know each of you had a life to which
You were as attached as each of us.
And too we know we each will one day,
Whether sooner or later,
Pass through this same exit.

We honor the great mystery of your death today
Which we witness in unknowingness.

For some of the many of us left here today without you,
The occasion of your death on this day
Is indelibly etched into our memory.
We shall remember the date of this day
For the rest of our lives.

To those of you who were aged,
We hope your departure provided relief
From infirmity, suffering, pain, and waiting.
We grieve with your loved ones.
We hope your final moments were filled
With rich memories of life,
And a mystical encounter with transcendence.
We celebrate your personal heroic odyssey, and
Thank you for what you gave.

To those of you who were in the prime of life,
Dying unexpectedly just as your purpose was maturing,
We mourn the loss of that which you were unable to complete.
Our hearts reach out to your loved ones
Who reel in shock and grief.

To those of you who were children,
We bear great sadness that
Your opportunity to grow was cut so short.
We will miss your joy and laughter and
The future you cannot now create.
If your death was caused by our neglect
And could have been prevented,
We reflect
And resolve to act anew.

To all of you in the passing stream of life,
We send our thoughts, our love, our respect.

December 1997

~

I Think It Is A Good Time To Die Now

I have known days.
I have been grateful for the glory and opportunity of 30,000 sunrises.
I have walked in awe in the shadow's stars.
I have felt the turning of my Earth,
Rolling, rolling,
Again and again.

I have known seasons.
I have rejoiced in Spring's renascence,
And celebrated Summer's profusion.
I have inhaled the sweet golds and crimsons of Fall,
And reflected in the virgin stillness of Winter's snow.
On this great circle around our blessed Star,
I have witnessed many processions of our axis.

I have known ages of being human.
I have passed through and witnessed
Infant innocence, youthful exuberance,
Young adult bravado, mid-aged aspiration,
Matured adulthood, wise elderhood, aging decay.
I have beheld the effects of the passage of time upon us,
From which none escape.

I have known the subtle mystery
Of existence,
And every beauteous being.
Of silence and music.
Of unending waves of breath.
Of realizing the Whole All.

I have known love and loved ones.
Work and disappointment.
Sorrows and joy.
Victory and hardship.

Yes…

You know, I think it's time to go now.
I think my purpose is complete here.
It's time to say my goodbyes to all I love,
And wholly melt back
Into the One.

October 1999

~

The Deepest Regret

Once I did not have time for you.
Now there is no more time.
Gone. Just like that.
Now you are gone from time.

I did not get to say goodbye to you.
I did not get to thank you.
I did not apologize to you.
I did not sing and dance and celebrate with you before you left time.

I think now of so much I did not do,
Now that I understand.
Too late.

I am sure you have forgiven me.
But I will live the rest of my life
With this regret.

I did not think you would die today,
So I did not do all this.
And now you are gone.
Gone.

September 1999

~

DEATH BY EARTHQUAKE

During the month of January, two earthquakes devastated the towns and villages of marginalized and impoverished people—one quake in El Salvador (officially killing a reported 2,000, but more likely 5,000-10,000); the other in western India (30,000 dead are officially reported, possibly 100,000 according to others; some deaths also occurred in Pakistan.)

I have died in millions of ultimately horrible ways—by starvation and torture, by painful disease and gruesome mutilation. I have gone down in planes, and been shot by death squads. I have been forced to witness the torment of my loved ones just before I was killed. I have been stranded in slow, impotent deaths.

It is not the *sudden* earthquake deaths, horrifying yet quick—but the excruciatingly slow deaths that can occur by earthquake which are perhaps the most horrible. Helplessly buried under tons of what was once one's home and valued possessions, but is suddenly termed *rubble*. Hearing the screams and cries for help of our loved ones, whom we cannot even contact or comfort. Hearing our loved ones, our children even, dying, again without being able to care for them. Painfully injured, but not mortally wounded; unable to move at all; listening for help and not knowing if ones' calls for help are entirely futile; lying in that gravity, with no light or food or water, often terribly cold, and with nothing—aware, heart beating, breathing, and watching one's life ever so slowly draining away. Having no concept of the passage of standard time as each moment extends to infinity, with nothing, absolutely nothing to do but contemplate how to meet the shock, the sorrow, the excruciating pain, the impotent helplessness, and the futile dilemma of whether to hope, struggle, or surrender. All around the area is the unheard but palpable enormity of grief, panic, fear, and emergency. Days can pass. *Days*! Each twenty-four hours is an eternity, and yet still lingering in suffering even more. And then, the putrid smell of the decaying flesh all around begins to seep into the living sepulcher. Oh god!

I have died millions of deaths, but I hate these deaths by earthquake.

On the day of the India quake (January 26) I recorded this, from my experience at the Salt Monument:

I wept with the grieved of the earthquake in India/Pakistan—all the scenes of grief, fear, horror, suffering, pain, uncertainty. I was orphaned, I lost my wife, my children, my husband, my parents, my friends, my home. I was buried alive in tons of rubble. I was the "lucky one" who *didn't* die of my family. Oh torments unlimited. I wept unendingly. I have died millions of deaths, but frankly, I hate the earthquake deaths. I went so far and so deep into so much grief, I was so weak I could hardly walk. And thereafter, life became so meaningless, I could only be in the simplest present.

The *added* tragedy in this is the role of poverty, greed, and inequity. "Natural disasters"— earthquakes, hurricanes, mudslides, drought, floods, etc.—do happen. These will always cause unavoidable deaths in catastrophic situations. But the deaths of *these* earthquakes were victims not of natural disaster per se, but of human negligence. These were people who were living in conditions that were patently, even knowingly, unsafe. In one of the El Salvador villages, the people had long been organizing against the deforestation and degradation of the hills above their homes. The danger of life-threatening mudslides was visible, foreseeable! The people in India are rallying to sue the various builders who constructed unsafe housing. A few hundred thousand people are *still*, today, homeless and mostly without food since the quake!

After the El Salvador quake, I wrote: I become the grief of a person whose loved ones have been missing for one week now. No more hope. My loved ones are under the mud, buried forever—I cannot even find their bodies. Grief unbearable. As that person (and thousands of others), my relationship to the soil of the Earth, which has swallowed up my family, is forever changed. I will never recover. Oh god! Oh god!

February 2001

~

WHERE ARE YOU?

THE SONG OF THOSE WHOSE LOVED ONE HAS DIED

Where are you, my beloved?
I have looked for you in my arms, but your arms no longer hold me.
I have looked for you in the forest of our courtship,
But you did not answer my call.
I have looked for you in my bed, but your warmth is no longer there.
Where, my love, where are you?
There are many stories people tell of where you have gone,
But they now seem only foolish palliatives to dissuade my grief.
My beloved, you are gone, gone from me forever,
Gone somehow where you can never be found to me again.

Where are you, my mother?
I am alone now in this world,
Far too young to be alone.
I have cried out to you,
But you no longer come to comfort me.
I cannot find you, I cannot see you,
I cannot hear you, I cannot touch you.
Where are you, my mother?
Where have you gone?

Where are you, my child?
Where are your eyes of innocence?
Your smile of purity?
Your laughter of hope?
Where is your future that I once saw laid out before you?
Where are you, my child?
I have looked for you in the garden, but I cannot find you there.
Where are you, my child?
Where have you gone?

December 1998

~

GONE, THE CONSTANT OF LIFE

Gone.
Gone from this life are my parents.
Gone too are my friends far away.
Gone is the warm embrace of my beloved.
Gone are so many of my hopes and dreams.

Gone is the life-filled forest I knew as a child.
Gone too the vast field.
Gone is the babbling stream which spoke the water blessing.
Gone the glittering songbirds declaring the morn.

Gone is my youthfulness.
Gone my eyesight.
Gone is my health and agility.
Gone my infant child.
Gone.

This is the constant of life.
Come to know it.
Come to love it.
For gone will all things be.
Gone, as the breath I breathe in
Must go out.
Gone as we each will be
As we let go our last breath.
Gone. Gone.

January 1999

~

On The Day I (You) Die

When we think of our own death,
We usually experience it as a singularity.
Yet, on the day each of us dies,
We die along with 150,00 other people.
Has anyone talked or thought about all those around the world
Who are dying with us as we are dying?
What would it be to actually remember this when dying?

February 1999

~

Thoughts On Human Sacrifice

It is something that even scholars admit they don't understand. There are prior cultures, most notably the Inca and Aztec, who regularly engaged in the practice of human sacrifice, usually of healthy children and teenagers. In the absence of written explanations of these rites, archaeologists find themselves truly perplexed as to its meaning, particularly in light of the extraordinarily high level of knowledge, culture, science, and government of these peoples. Dumbfounded, we ask of this obvious abomination of moral/ethical behavior: Why did they do this?

Who could take a beautiful young child and intentionally murder them in front of others? Why would parents be honored to offer their own child for this fate? Why would the remains of those sacrificed show that they were neither afraid nor forced? What beliefs in the afterlife would bring such indifference or even reverence of death?

I ask: What if there is an entirely different way of seeing this?

Death is the most powerful teacher we have. Ask anyone who has survived a so-called *near death experience*. Death is the most certain thing about life—it is something to which we are all equally destined. Yet for most of us, we live in near constant denial of the reality of death and its ever-present nature. In any and every given moment, the veil between life and death can be parted instantly…irreversibly. How many of us live in that awareness?

At the Salt Monument, we become observers of the constant flow. Birth to death, birth to death. Everyone who is here was once born, is now somewhere along the path of that journey, and will at some time die. In a civilization that is conscious, there is great awareness of this. The flow. It is the flow that becomes the guideline of meaning. The individual itself in this context becomes much less significant. When we are truly committed to our heritage and realistic about our shared fate, the individual drama of our personal existence is much less significant. This is the traditional, albeit natural, realization in any village of humans, where the birth/life/death cycle is evident and inescapable. Of course in the American/Western contemporary culture, we hold individual life as highly significant, even most important. People rarely offer themselves up for sacrifice here.

And yet...

If we observe honestly, we will see that the effect of human sacrifice is still in operation (both intentional and unintentional sacrifice), is quite powerful, and has the ability to shift awareness or deeply galvanize people more than any other form of teaching.

For example, the sacrifice two thousand years ago of a man we call Jesus is *still* having the most profound impact. Socrates sacrificed his life for philosophy. The sacrifice of the (relatively) young leaders, John Kennedy and Martin Luther King Jr., made them and their values/impact immeasurably more powerful than if they had lived. Human sacrifice—called *public execution*—has been practiced for thousands of years in virtually every culture, and is even to this day done in the United States (though the rest of the *civilized* world banned it) under the clinical reference: *death penalty*. Princess Diana's death was a sacrifice shockingly demonstrating the perils of public adulation. Recently, the heinous shooting spree of two students at a high school in Colorado sorrowfully sacrificed fifteen people. Yet this one incident brought untold awareness of the urgent needs of our youths—needs which were equally great and well-documented though largely ignored prior to the gruesome incident.

Sacrifice affects us. It is most affecting when the young are lost to death. It wakes us up from delusion and complacency. It reminds us of the sacredness of life, the holy bonds between us and our loved ones, the fragility of our time and lives, the meanings which are deeper than our individual desires, the value of our interdependence. Sacrifice is a powerful teacher which permanently brands itself into our hearts and minds.

I am not implying that the ancient practices of sacrifice were not mired in superstition, religiosity, and ignorance. However, it is possible that the origins were supremely wise.

What if the Inca and Aztec sacrifices were based on a great depth of thought? What if—rather than waiting for the random chance of sacrifice to occur in order to remind us of the remarkable gift of life and the sacredness of our society—what if a people saw that creating this as an infrequent but regular, completely conscious and intentional ceremony could inspire a depth of awareness that could scarcely be more affecting?

From that standpoint, it is easy to see how offering oneself or a loved one would be regarded as a great privilege. If done in true consciousness, it would indicate genuine understanding of the reality of life and death—the willingness to give of oneself, to *sacrifice* one's own individual self for the benefit of many others, not for the glory but in the knowing that we are all going to die anyway. There is hardly a nobler position to take. Belief in a literal after-life is irrelevant from this standpoint. When the known effect of one's life is the inspiration and upliftment of one's whole society, that in itself is a life worth living and dying. Besides, the greatest fear about death is the unknowing: not knowing when or how or how painful, unexpected, inglorious it may be dealt us. The person who allows themselves to be sacrificed is relieved of all such fear. (And it should be noted that the Inca/Aztec sacrifices, based on the facial expressions of the bodies found, were conducted painlessly and even perhaps pleasantly.)

The world *sacrifice* comes from the Latin: *to make sacred*.

I recently heard a tape of Alan Watts where he quoted Jean-Paul Sartre as saying: "The only real philosophical question is whether to commit suicide or not." I realize that very few people will understand that comment, but at the very least Sartre, Watts, and I did.

It is an extraordinarily pithy summation.

November 1999

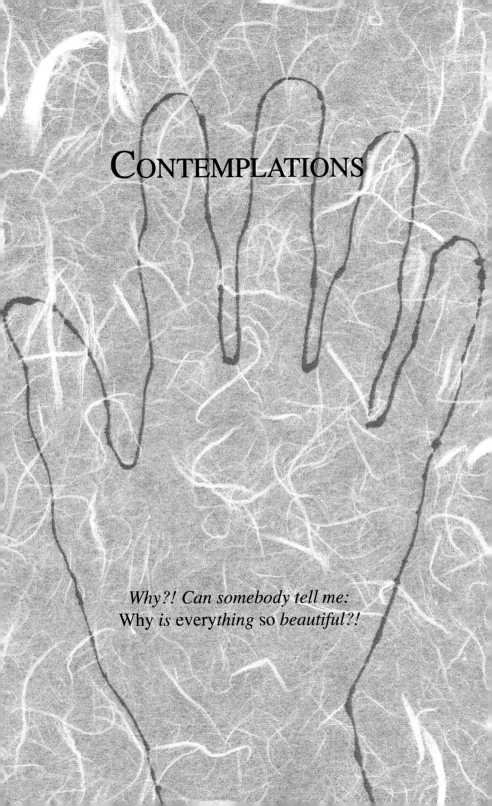

CONTEMPLATIONS

Why?! Can somebody tell me:
Why is everything so beautiful?!

~

Prayer Of Gratitude

As infinite as the cause of breath,
Such is the prayer of gratitude.

I have tried to conceive all my gratitude—
From the mundane to the sublime.
Each day I thank my body for its functioning,
My bed for the blessing of safe and peaceful rest,
The food which sustains me,
The many people whose labor supports me,
The atmosphere which protects me,
The turning Earth which brings day and night,
The great Sun upon which we depend,
The vast Galaxy that birthed us.
Ah, I have tried to conceive all my gratitude...
But I always find I have scarce begun.

I have tried to cry all my gratitude—
For the blessings I am given both great and small.
Each day I cry in thanks for the simple freedom I know,
For the grace and comforts of my life,
I cry with gratitude that I am not
Starving or impoverished,
In pain or oppressed,
As so many others of my human family unjustly are.
Ah, I have tried to cry all my gratitude...
But I always find I have scarce begun.

I have tried to smile all my gratitude—
For the beauty and the miracle.
Each day I smile in thanks to the living beings all around me,
The people and birds, the insects and trees.
To the colors of life and its endless creativity,
To the wonder of water, and light,
To the infinite within and the infinite without,
To the blessing of loved ones,
To the mystery of birth and death.
Ah, I have tried to smile all my gratitude…
But I always find I have scarce begun.

September 1999

~

UNIQUENESS

Like so many snowflakes,
So are we.
Each beautiful,
Infinitely unique from any other
Ever before or after.

Exquisite and ephemeral,
We are born as an incomparable snowflake,
Fated wholly to dissolve.
It is very simple.

October 1999

$\backsim$

To Comprehend The Incomprehensible

This is the purpose of the Salt Monument: to bring an incomprehensible reality into the context of some semblance of comprehensibility.

What does it actually mean to be one single individual among six billion others? To comprehend the incomprehensible, let us stand before six billion and truly see ourselves in context.

What does it mean to stand on the huge, beauteous Earth and know it is a tiny fleck in a vast emptiness?

There is each day a dawn. But it is not enough to only gaze in rapture upon the glory of another dawn and then another, to revel in the return of light, to drink in the resplendent color, to celebrate the hope of another day. For what is it to really feel the Earth rolling in space and circling our endless path? To see myself as a microscopic speck on this so-huge-to-me water planet where billions of trillions of other living beings also receive the dawn? What is it to comprehend the enormity of this our Sun/star? To feel ourselves hurtling along with our Sun and all the stars we see in a 500,000 mile per hour whirlwind galaxy whose movement is so vast we cannot detect it whatsoever, and yet even still know that this, our galaxy, is a mere fleck in a universe of such immensity we cannot ever comprehend?!

I press my thoughts and feelings and awareness ever further, ever further, knowing I cannot, I can never comprehend the incomprehensible. To try and ever know I fail to pass beyond even the limitations of comprehension is to know the incomprehensible.

It is not enough to be grateful for this water so easily flowing out from this faucet, but to seek to feel, to know: that water cradles our planet by 75% of its surface, that all the water that is also was and ever will be here, that we live on islands, that this mysterious substance is the primal ingredient of every living thing, that huge lakes dwell untouched beneath us in ancient aquifers, that here are two gasses mysteriously fused, that this miracle is the same as ice, blood, tears, snow, clouds, everywhere connecting us to everything and everyone. It is good to take a few moments as I wash my hands to be grateful for this water. But what if I strive to comprehend the incomprehensible miracle and mystery of water?

It is good to take a moment to send a message of love to all of humanity...But what is it to see each one as me, to honor each person's life full of hope and disappointment, of birth/growth/aging/death? What is it to know that each who is young today will be old, that each who is old was once youthful? What is it to feel each and every one in their all-important acts of selfhood, their waking and sleeping, their suffering and victories, their drudgery and glory? What is it to know that each one of us is a peculiar bag of water and cooperative republic of sixty trillion cells, each *cell* silently fulfilling *their* individual destiny?

It is good to be kind to those with whom I engage every day—my family, my friends, the people whose paths I cross in the mundane comings and goings of a day. But what is it to look through each of their eyes into the depths of their being and to connect in a divine moment of oneness? What is it to remember that for certain either they will live to see me die or I they? What is it to transcend the limitations of time and know that this man was so recently a little boy with little boy dreams and fears, soon to be a corpse, and that this little girl is so soon a mother of children? What is it to honor the miracle of embodiment, that somehow in this enormously empty universe, we happen to encounter another living being?

It is not enough to be thankful in the simple buying this thing— this food, this clothing, this gasoline, this whatever—nor to realize in gratitude the great privilege of having any money at all with which to buy it. For what is it to feel the thousands upon thousands of hands that have touched this thing, or to see the miles upon miles of lands and oceans it has passed through? What is it to perceive the myriad impacts on people, places, living beings to have brought this thing to me, or to realize the vast and complex network of interdependence that wove this thing from a thousand sources?

What is it to strive to comprehend the incomprehensible? It is thankless, endless, and inherently impossible. My sparce words and thoughts here give scarcely a glimpse and yet already far exceed any possibility of comprehension. Still, this is my work to which I am ever devoted.

To comprehend the incomprehensible.

March 1999

~

MEDITATION ON THE SOUND OF ALL

As I chant *ohm*, I am joined into the river of all sound.
It is the sound of every person who is just now singing,
Or speaking, or chanting, or moaning, or crying, or laughing.
In the *ohm* I hear all the people everywhere in the sound
       they are making.

In the *ohm* is the sound of every living being expressing itself just now.
It is the sound of every bird singing, dog barking,
       monkey screeching, elephant trumpeting, tree branch cracking,
       flower unfolding, bee and fly buzzing.
In the *ohm* I hear all the beings everywhere on Earth
       in the sound they are making.

In the *ohm* is the sound of water flowing, trickling, waving,
       falling, raining, snowing, dripping—
       water sounding everywhere on this great planet.
In the *ohm* I hear the mysterious sound of the planets spinning,
       of the supernovas exploding, of the great galaxies unfurling.
In the *ohm* is heard the sound of all.

As I intone the bell, I am joined into the river of the sounds
       created by the things which human beings made.
I hear the machines whirring, the clanging of tools, the jets roaring,
       the wheels rolling, the computers purring, the musical instruments
       transforming human voice/sound into other dimensions.
In the toning of the bell, I am joined into the river of all sounds
       created by the hands and minds of humans.

The sound of all.
Oh yes.
It is another dimension of incomprehensibility.

March 1999

~

Reality Is Wordless

We are so driven, defined, and entrapped by words, the quite obvious truth escapes us:

Reality is wordless.

Words are the invention of human thinking. Reality is most certainly not the invention of human thinking. Thus it is absurd to expect that we can use words to define or understand reality.

The only way we can even begin to comprehend reality is to become wordless ourselves.

In some ways we see this in the infant's wisdom, which we so often acknowledge, before language inundates thought. But for true realization, we need both the infant's wisdom and the learned mystic, combining sagacious knowledge, skill, experience, and expansion into wordless reflection, absorption, responsiveness, and openness.

Words are of humans. The *energy* of language can be witnessed in the communication of other creatures, even at the cellular level, even (more esoterically) at the sub-atomic level. There is communication in these (i.e. the exchange of perceptions) *but* it is not in *words*.

I love that the Salt Monument is wordless. In this, it bypasses all human mental constructs and lies precisely in the realm of reality.

March 1999

~

THERE *ARE* EXTRAORDINARY GRAINS OF SALT—
EQUALITY, RELEVANCE, AND RARITY

Upon looking at six billion grains of salt representing us, we are struck by the similarity and uniformity of those crystals. The very idea of the Salt Monument is to represent us as equals. But the truth is, we are no more equals as human beings than we are as grains of salt. Once again, ubiquitously enough, we find: our perception of equality is not truth but rather is subjectively a result of the scale/dimension/faculties from and with which we are observing. In other words, grains of salt are as different from one another as human beings are. Just as we cannot make out any uniqueness or differences whatsoever among people from a distance of a few miles (if we can even see them), so are we unable to detect the myriad uniqueness among grains of salt without the benefit of a magnifying glass, or even better a microscope. It is only a matter of proximity or distance that gives us the illusion of similarity or uniqueness. Relevance also plays a part.

Myself, I have personally observed millions upon millions of grains of salt. During the past twenty months, I have seen over 80 million individual grains of salt pass before my eyes into water, representing those who have died in the world. I have seen nearly 200 million individual grains of salt poured into receptacles representing those who were born. I have also meticulously counted thousands of grains of salt.

I can tell you this: there *are* extraordinary grains of salt. In all of those 300 million or so grains who I have personally observed, I can actually remember a few remarkable and distinct grains of salt. There have been perhaps twenty or thirty of a particularly unique type which were very large, round and opaque white. I once saw one that was strangely shaped and amber-toned; I have never seen another like it.

This is profoundly similar to what I observe is the actual occurrence among human beings. There simply *are* extraordinary human beings. However much we may want to include all of us as equals, there simply are a few people who stand out as undeniably, remarkably exceptional.

Then there is the plain fact that when we look under a microscope at each grain of salt—as with a snowflake, as with a person—we will find that each one is utterly and entirely unique. Although this is a very sticky distinction for some to make, there *is* a difference between the ultimate divine uniqueness of each individual-anything and the observation that among any grouping of anythings there may be truly exceptional individuals based on the rarity of one sort of occurrence or characteristic or another.

Again, the degree to which this is of any significance whatsoever is strictly a matter of scale and relevance.

For example, let us look across the grasses carpeting these hundred acres in our view. There are many, many blades of grass to be seen in this one visual sweep. It could surely be a billion or two (or more.) When you and I look at these blades of grass, we will tend to lump them all together into one equality: these are all blades of grass. However it is certain that among these two billion blades of grass there are one or two who are utterly remarkable as far as blades of grass go. Perhaps they grew faster and sooner than any others. Perhaps they are taller, thinner, or greener. Perhaps they have a special resistance to any intruding pest. Perhaps their curve is an entirely unique innovation. Nevertheless, to you and I, the exceptional nature of those two blades of grass among those billions is entirely irrelevant. We cannot be bothered to single them out, and even if we did, it would hardly matter to us. Who really cares about an exceptional blade of grass? Whether we introduce this blade of grass to a person riding the subway in New York City, a whale swimming in the Pacific, or even to a caterpillar (who likes to eat blades of grass), its exceptional nature is wholly immaterial to each of them.

So it is with us, although again this may not be a popular conclusion. We must be honest in realizing there genuinely are unprecedented, rare individuals who appear among the multitude of humanity and are notable as exceptions in one way or another. At the same time, we must recognize that beyond the proximity of the teensy human scale of time and space, this is utterly irrelevant. And too, at the same time, we must acknowledge that within our own tiny dimension, each and every individual is utterly unique and deserving of honor as such. When we can hold all this simultaneously and harmoniously, then we begin to approach an understanding of equality, relevance, and rarity.

Postscript. It should be noted, one week later, during the daily birth ceremony, I witnessed a truly remarkable single grain of salt as it was added to the 1700 pound body of the Salt Monument. I actually saw this one, larger, distinctive pinkish grain fall as if in slow motion from the birth stream onto the mound—it was *that* noticeable to capture my attention! In my musings on this, I let that single grain represent a truly significant human being who was born on that day, unbeknownst to the billions of others. In retrospect, we celebrate the birth day of a great person—there are many examples of this. In retrospect, we even concoct stories of the auspicious signs and the awareness of the elite on the day when a special person was born (i.e. the birth stories of Jesus and Buddha). Actually witnessing the realistic context of such a birth created an entirely new perspective of such an event. I saw what a far and long journey a newborn has to go before they can become who they are and make their impact and contribution; the innumerable many others they must coexist with; the vast unknown obstacles, challenges, and perils they must endure in order to fulfill their destiny.

On that morning, I allowed myself to celebrate that birth as if I were truly privy to the knowledge that an extraordinary savior of humankind was born that day. I glorified that single birth in dance, song, and ecstasy; I toasted to the heavens for such a gift; I stood gaping in awe at the one single amazing grain among six billion; I fervently pressed blessings onto that infant's future, hoping that they will be able to surpass all the obstacles to come; I realistically understood the enormous odds against them achieving their fate.

On the very next day, the grains of the next influx of newborns buried that remarkable grain and thus it was joined in the great mass of humanity. Most likely, I will never see that single grain of salt again.

Let it be stated here, if twenty or more years from now we notice that someone incredibly remarkable *was* actually born on May 23, 1999, here is evidence that their greatness was truly foretold. Now wouldn't *that* make a good story!?

However, and regardless, the truth and joy is in the play of it.

May 1999

~

Ourself and Our Self

We are all always thinking of ourselves.
This is natural and unavoidable.
Our only hope is to redefine the *meaning* of our self.

When we redefine our self as *every*one.
Then, not only are we in realization of the True Self,
But then we are also always thinking of everyone.

When our Self includes everyone and everything,
Then we are complete and completely at Peace.

July 1999

~

TWO CERTAINTIES

Good Morning, again. It always happens. (A new morning, that is.) It is so amazing. Think about it. There are two things we can depend on: the sun will rise (and set), and we each will die. Beyond that just about everything else is uncertain. This is why many have worshipped the Sun; it is the closest available parallel to the characteristics of the Divine: constant, unchangeable, non-judgmental, life-giving, all-embracing, all-whatever. This is also why the idea of a special person who goes beyond death by being an immortal or having a resurrection after death is so deeply needed by people. Our death brings us a face-to-face certainty with what we cannot control. It forces our surrender and it shows us our limitations: we are indeed *very* finite. This is not a desired realization for most of us. So we conceive people who are above and beyond death, and we conceptualize reincarnation and more. It does have truth in it, just as all our spiritual stories have allegorical and symbolic truth imbedded in them. But to consider them literally is a denial of our universal certainty.

May 1999

~

INDIVIDUATION AS DROPS OF WATER

Water is such an apt metaphor to bring virtual illustration to many understandings.

In the ocean waves we see drops flung into the air, which then fall down and back into the water. What a great way to see individual identity. For our brief millisecond of life, we are flung into our individuated body, we go on the *wheeee* ride of life. We truly appear as a single, independent, dynamic identity—individual, unique, with our own trajectory and path. We are still part of the ocean, we are still the same water; it is just that we momentarily (and validly) appear separate. Eventually we reach our peak and succumb to the gravity of dissolution. Then it is time to let go and fall back into the oneness. Poof. Within seconds (no matter how high we flew), we are dissolved back into our origin, our oneness, our non-distinguishable-ness.

We spend our lives identifying with our self, developing it, catering to it, fulfilling it—only to find: it was all an illusion and nothing. As individuals we are so very close to nothing. All that fuss about our own individual life, and in the end we are simply, unnoticeably, irreversibly, and so tiny-ly dissolved in a vast body of All.

September 1999

~

Now Is: Contemplation On Time

If we are honest and clear we will see,
Most of life occurs in either memory or imagination.
The only *real* part is the passing through—
A tiny point of light moving always.

Time flows and
              is like a person
                    is like a galaxy
                          is like a stream.

We call each of these a *thing*, as if it exists.
But in truth each is just a passing through,
A phenomenon of change through time
That has some pattern
Which we recognize as consistent.

Just as a galaxy is something we observe through time
(That is, what we see happened a billion years ago, or
One side of it is 100,000 years older than the other)
So we can see a person through time.
In their present moment,
We can see them as the pattern of all their prior ages,
As well as those yet to come.
There is only one time and one thing: Now Is.

September 1999

~

There Is Only One Day

There is only one day, and it has already lasted billions and billions of years.

When we really observe what is going on here, we see this so clearly. There is no *today* or *tomorrow* for the Earth. There is a constant half-circle of sunlight, a constant half-circle of shadow, and a never-ending border where the two meet—all of which are in constant motion and have always been for five billion years or so. This is an actual reality.

The concept of a twenty-four hour day arises from the extremely local perspective of staying at one spot and observing the *illusion* of sun*rise* and sun*set*. *Today* is something we share with the beings in our locale, but otherwise it is hard to find *today*. If we listen this moment to people around the planet, they will say: "Now is sunrise…No, now is *my* sunset…It is noon here…It is night here…Now it is sunset…No, now is my *sunrise*…" It just goes on and on. Some people are waking while another's day is ending. Noon here, midnight there. Then we switch. Ongoing, ever ongoing. It never stops.

The deceit of *today* and *tomorrow* can be revealed when we consider the mark on a globe which is called "the international date line." In order to make sense to our linear viewpoint, *people* drew an imaginary line from the North Pole to South Pole and we said: On this side we will call it *today*, and on that side we will call it *tomorrow*. Notice that in order to avoid the obvious confusion about all this, this line was drawn in the middle of the hugest ocean on the planet, i.e. where the fewest people would be affected by its necessary absurdity.

There is only one day and it is already five billion years long. The contemplation of this is a vast dimension. One time, in meditation of this on the field, I actually became that one day all throughout all Earth time—I heard/felt/became it. It was an awesomeness indescribable.

It should at least be mentioned that similarly: there is no birth, no death—there is only one life. But we'll leave that for another time.

November 1999

~

Consciousness Of Self As One Organism

Just as there is a consciousness of a person that perceives ourself to be one single organism, despite the fact that we are actually sixty trillion independent beings (i.e. cells) operating in consort, so is there a consciousness of Life that perceives itself as a single being or Oneness, despite the fact that it is actually billions of trillions of independent beings (i.e. creatures).

One interesting thing about our consciousness is that although we are aware of our*self* as a totality, we are unaware of our individual units. For example, our individual consciousness is not able to clearly perceive the activities of individual cells in our body. Except when considerable disturbance occurs, we are mostly and utterly unconscious of the functions, locations, activities, and even well-being of *any* of our sixty trillion cells. We can even try very hard to be aware of a single cell and find this next to impossible, even with great focus, effort, and mastery.

If we extrapolate this to the supposition of a consciousness of the entire self of Life on Earth, then it would correspond that although we, as individual Life creatures, are fully aware of our activities/functions/well-being, the consciousness of Life—although filled with an awareness of itself at a level which we cannot comprehend (just as any individual cell of our body could *never* comprehend the consciousness by which we define our *self*)—is unaware of individual creatures. This actually makes enormous sense, although admittedly I can see how one might get lost in my words here.

Further, there is a similar consciousness even into further units of organization, i.e. solar system, galaxy, supercluster, etc. up to the total Cosmos which also follows this pattern. If we continued to take this to its extreme, we will come to an ultimate Universal Consciousness, the *Whole All*, but—contrary to all our usual assumptions/imaginings that such an all-encompassing Consciousness would have awareness of absolutely *everything*—we will find that although its awareness does encompass everything, it is utterly *un*aware of *anything*!

Thus it is when we absorb ourselves in the consciousness of Life or the Ultimate, we become unaware of our individual human consciousness (i.e. we *transcend* personal self-identification) and are subsumed into a larger Self.

September 1998

~

THE SUB-MICROSCOPIC EARTH
WITHIN THE SEA OF GALAXIES

If you and I were to take a drop of water from a vital pond and
peer into it through a powerful microscope, we would witness a
world of life. We could observe thousands, even millions and billions (if our microscope was really powerful), of living beings—
swimming, reproducing, eating, utilizing one another in myriad
ways, dying, traveling, and so on. If we watched over time, we
might see empires of one sort of creature rise up and dominate
the others, or we might see one group proliferate until it had de-
pleted its food sources and despoiled its niche.

We might watch with a sense of wonder and yet detachment,
vaguely aware of our preeminent Olympian vantage and slight
disdain for those creatures' microscopic insignificance.

We live in a drop of water in the pond of our solar system.

Our Earth is proportionally as enormous to us as a drop of water
to the sub-microscopic beings. Yet on the scale of galaxies, even
the seeming enormity of our entire solar system is itself sub-
microscopic! We smugly view the bacteria swimming in our pond
with our sense of superiority and importance in the universe. How
blatantly in error we are.

In our spiritual musings, we so often view ourselves, whether subtly or overtly, as the purpose of the universe, a monumental manifestation of consciousness within the known universe. We imagine the angels and gods of the universe ministering to our thoughts and actions. We conjure up superior beings from other galaxies who are engrossed with our progress and dabble in our process.

Yet, we are so infinitesimal within this Universe, our insignificance is incomprehensible to us. To the same degree that we can witness the submicroscopic beings in our drop of pond water and confidently state that they have no idea whatsoever who *we* are, how we are observing them, and all of the what-else is happening on this Earth of which we are so knowledgeable—to this same degree are we oblivious to and incapable of comprehending what we do not know and how small *we* truly are.

April 1998

~

Oh, Salt! Pure, Immortal

Oh course,
And it is never mentioned.

Salt:

Pure.
Immortal.
The Atman of each.

Dissolved,
But never gone.

September 2000

All Life Is Sacred

ALL life is sacred.
Every, every, every bit of life is absolutely sacred.

Why?

Because Life is a miracle
In the Universe.

October 2000

~

THE MACROCOSMIC/MICROCOSMIC CONTINUUM

We just happen to be located somewhere along the continuum of scale between the macrocosmic and the microcosmic. Within any set of things along that continuum—whether sub-atomic particles, single-cells, complex organisms, solar systems, galaxies, supra-galactic systems—any set is equally complex, intelligent, inter-related, and self-absorbed as any other. Sixty trillion beings on Earth are just as engaged in being who they are as the sixty trillion cells which comprise one human being or the sixty trillion stars which comprise a galactic cluster.

Where one happens to find oneself along the continuum is irrel-evant. The conditions are still the same. Whatever the relative di-mension—whether subatomic or macrocosmic—all things tend to operate in general oblivion or necessary disregard for all things beyond that specific scale.

I saw a tiny spider today. This spider was so small as to be imper-ceptible—a tiny red dot smaller than the period at the end of this sentence—-*smaller* than a grain of salt. I only knew this was a living being because my visual attention perceived the movement on the bathroom counter as I brushed my teeth—a tiny red ball rolling around on the inert surface. This insect lives in a different dimension of time, space, and purpose than we do—in a reality specific to its own locus. Within that reality, the tiny spider's re-connoitering of that enormous surface was fully in earnest. Yet it is so easy for us to see this creature's meandering as senseless, inconsequential, even foolhardy. I watched the spider roaming back and forth in circles, going nowhere in particular. It is so easy for us to dismiss this creature's existence as insignificant. Is this because it is so small? To us, an insect's minute travels are so easily viewed as aimless, irrelevant, unnoticeable, and quite obviously, vastly ignorant. Yet until I noticed this tiny living being, I was entirely absorbed in the specific reality of my own locus, equally oblivious to this creature, to its unknown mission, to the mysteries of its history and ancestry.

Are we not as limited by *our* locus as the spider? Captivated by our own world, in our own dimension of space and time, in our own sensory functions, are we not just as oblivious and ignorant of that which we cannot even begin to comprehend—the constant gyrations of subatomic particles, the submicroscopic worlds within us, the eons of time on this planet, the vastness of space, the movements of our galaxy? From the perspective of the universe, we can immediately realize: all of our history, technology, brilliance, self-awareness, knowledge, and wisdom—all this, from the perspective of the universe, can too be seen as aimless, irrelevant, unnoticeable, and quite obviously, vastly ignorant, minute traipsing. Perhaps we too are so small as to be irrelevant.

From the viewpoint of the Sun, our Earth appears as a teensy ball and we humans—with all our heroic explorations and grand accomplishments—appear far, far smaller than this spider.

In our minds, is it only size that determines importance? If we dismiss this tiny spider as insignificant and worthless, then mustn't we conclude: in the context of the universe, we are ourselves entirely insignificant and worthless? If instead we recognize our similarity and equality with this tiny spider, doesn't it change our conception of ourselves and our universe?

October 1997

~

I Stand In Awe Of My Insignificance

I am insignificant among my human family. When I see myself among six billion others, I realize my delusion. I sit before six billion grains of salt and try to comprehend that I am as one grain among those many. I cannot conceive this, and even less that billions have come and gone before, and billions are yet to come— even within my own lifetime! There are so many people. I am among an invisible, voiceless multitude. I was born. I will do my best in life. I will die. I am nothing but another one among billions of human beings that come and go. Among my human family, I have no significance except to myself and a small handful of others. I am one-six-billionth of humanity, as are you. I can scarcely be found among us. Before the multitude of humanity, I stand in awe of my insignificance.

I am insignificant among earthly creatures. Although my human family numbers nearly six billion, humans are utterly insignificant in true relation to the trillions upon trillions of other beings with whom we share this planet. *Our* world view has us believe we are the masters. In truth, we are fledgling newcomers, far outnumbered by a vast majority of others who held dominion on the planet long before our arrival. I cannot comprehend nor truly contact even just the beetles of our planet, who comprise fully 25% of all species who live here, let alone the trillions of insects (representing over half of all creatures). Among the gigantic family of Life, I am so insignificant, I can hardly be noticed.

I am insignificant to my Earth. The vastness of this rock in space is so incomprehensible to me, I spend most of my life in complete ignorance of this simple fact. I cling to the tiny patch of soil on which I enact my life dramas, yet to the Earth, my existence is so vastly insignificant, it feels absurd when it is even glimpsed.

I am insignificant in time. *Billions* of years. We speak of four and five billions of years in the discussions of Life's and the Earth's timeframes. These are easy terms to throw around. For about three billion years, life developed strictly on a microscopic scale. How long really is a billion years? Let us be truthful in our hubris. Even as a human family, we scarcely exist in time. As individuals, our insignificance in time is self-defining. My whole life span is less than a trillionth of a millisecond in the scale of this planet.

I am insignificant in space. We have peered into the visible universe to a distance of eleven billion *light years*. Again, these are words we toss about and use to sound intelligent. But what really is a light year? In itself, this is a distance so beyond our comprehension, it is the very reason we devised the measurement—a light year is a distance so huge, it is not measurable in any relatable terms. My teensy traipsing through space, even including the billions of miles' journey I hitch on my ride on our planet's solar orbit, is wholly negligible in the context of true universal space.

I stand deeply in awe. There is something sublime in truly realizing one's insignificance. To see oneself as the nothing which one is, in its most profound dimensions, is not only terribly humbling, it is also ultimately realistic. Further, in the emptiness that I become in realizing my insignificance, I enter the insignificance/significance of All.

November 1997

~

Dimensions

SCROLL AT THE SALT MONUMENT

There are many galaxies in the Universe.
And on Earth:
There are many drops of water.
There are many rocks.
There are many trees.
There are many insects.
There are many people.
There are many cells.
There are many DNA molecules.

December 1999

~

Transcendence: An Analogy

Our deeper self can be likened to the Earth,

Rolling

...ceaselessly

...steadily

...intently

All the trillion myriad happenings, beings, and fluctuations
Invariably happening on the surface
Do nothing,
Nothing,

To perturb this constancy.

October 2000

~

VOID AS THE UNIVERSAL CONSTANT

Given the current knowledge of our universe, it is calculated: for every atom in the universe, there are 88 gallons of space. This would be similar to finding nothing whatsoever except *one* grain of salt in an entirely empty vacuum of five thousand cubic miles everywhere you went! How fascinating!

For one, it points to the extraordinary rarity of having what we call a "physical form." From the one-atom-to-88-gallons-of-space ratio, the truly remarkable thing in the universe is to be any *thing* whatsoever. To rephrase it, we could say: to *not* be *nothing* is extremely rare. Because we are so absorbed and captive in our own human/Earth localized scale here, we erroneously feel inundated with *thingness*. There are so many *things*, so much diversity, so much manifestation. Everywhere we look, every way we feel, is connected to thingness—whether that of our own and others' bodies, or anything about the world in which we live. We have thus concluded that being a *thing* of any sort is not that special. In fact, many people of many spiritual leanings have spent many thousands of years attempting to release themselves from their *physical form* because they have felt it was inferior to a non-physical form. Nothing could be further from the truth. Even to be the sun, or any other star, or a 100,000-light-years-diameter galaxy, even to be the entirety of a super-cluster of galaxies…even at this enormous, incomprehensible scale, physical existence is an exceptional rarity.

Further still, to actually be a living/organic/creature/being/human— capable of comprehending, discovering, and realizing all this—is one of the rarest and greatest opportunities of the universe! Yet we, in our limited viewpoint, seek to be released of this *cumbersome* existence!

The atom-to-space ratio also demonstrates the enormous absolute unknowable-ness of the great Void. In the absence of *any* matter, what is always there is the great darkness: the Void. It is a darkness that is so mysteriously vast, it entirely swallows the massive lights of the trillions upon trillions of brilliant, hot, unimaginably intense stars. The darkness, the emptiness, the no-thing-ness is so huge, no amount of thing-ness can come anywhere close to even remotely denting its mastery of all. The void, the emptiness, exists even within us on such a vast scale—subatomically—that it is said we would be one-millionth the size of a grain of salt were all the space to be removed from our own body!

Void is a constant. Whether in the macrocosmic dimension or the microscopic or subatomic, void's consistently extensive presence is in all, at all layers of scale. 99.999...% of all *matter* is *void*! This is observable in every dimensional context, whether we examine the solar system, a galaxy, the universe, a creature, a cell, or the subatomic realms. In every single instance, the void is dominant and substance is the rarity at any given scale, *except* within the very narrow band at which we operate. Once again, it brings that awareness of the rarity and privilege of being material, although we often consider the disembodied as a *higher* state of existence. In truth, about the only advantage of disembodiment for human beings is the absence of desire and suffering.

September 1998

≈

SACRED SPACE

Sacred space.
Where, ah, where?
Where can I find sacred space?
In a world filled with disregard and unrest,
Where shall I find sanctity and peace?

I look within my very body:
And find here mysteries upon mysteries
Unfathomable;
Vast expanses and ceaseless waves;
Profound and inexplicable.

I take a single step:
And *wherever* I am,
I walk upon a billions-year-old relic;
Temple of unimaginable beauty;
The shrine of all known life.

I look into your eyes:
And here I see
Eons of humanity—
Countless cycles of joys and sorrows;
The silent miracle of love.

Where? Where indeed
Shall I find sacred space?
It is every breath I breathe.
It is every step I take.
It is every one I meet.
It is every thing I am.
It is here.

October 2001

OUR WORLD

Let us realize the reality of our magnificent planet…
And see ourselves in true perspective of:
The trillions of other creatures,
The billions of Earth years,
The untold light-years of our Universe.

~

ANOTHER DAY

Another day of birth and death,

Of joy and sorrow,

Of horror and wonder.

Another day/night

Of Earth rolling.

Another day.

March 2002

~

GAIA'S HUMILITY

So humble is the Earth.

In the great and unfathomable expanse of space…in the presence of countless vast galactic bodies…near the glory of exploding nebula…in the darkness between the hundreds of billions of nearby stars…held in place by the invisible power of one great star/Sun…

Amidst all this, floats a tiny molecule—our Earth.

From the perspective of all that enormity, the Earth is so inconsequential as to be irrelevant. Its place amid the Universe is humble beyond all humility.

Imagine if the Earth was aware of itself within the context of the actual Universe in which it exists. How might it feel and know itself?

So small, so humble, so honestly diminished as it gazes sincerely into the vastness, the brilliance, the power, the majestic enigma. But this humility does nothing to negate the magic, the miracle, the beauty, the preciousness of the Earth's form, processes, and life. It is just that there is nothing boastful about the Earth.

In the great Void, the Earth is a rare and tiny jewel…outshone, outnumbered, outdone in every way by all that is around it. Even still, humble as it may be, its exquisiteness is undeniable. In simply being what it is, it is extraordinary.

January 1999

~

Globe-Portrait Of Our Earth

I had long searched for a *real* globe—a globe that would depict the Earth as seen from space, with no words written on it, with actual color, with realistic cloud cover. There was none to be found. Finally, the only solution was to *paint* a globe.

The act of painting a globe is filled with teaching and profound insights about life, Earth, history, reality, humanity…everything. And it is so indicative of the human state of mind that no one is making/wants/needs the *true reality* globe—we want the *human distinction* globe.

The process of painting the globe itself created a remarkable meditation about our planet. In order to fully *erase* the words, I found the best solution was to apply a generous layer of gesso (white medium) onto the surface. In order to preserve the detail, I found it was best to first gesso the oceans, paint them blue, and then gesso the landforms and paint them. It was a painstaking process, involving hours of close detailed tracing with a tiny brush *twice* around myriad boundaries—first the edges of water meeting land and then the same again for the edges of land meeting water.

In the process of it, I observed how little I know about my planet. Oceans upon oceans of which I am completely unaware. Hundreds of countries I could not even come close to finding, were it not for the words on the globe. Ignorant. I saw how ignorant I am. I know we invest considerable time in educating our children about *geography*. Why? There is a reason. As children, it is incomprehensible that there are really people and places so different and so far away from our immature and tiny locus of perception. So we try to educate ourselves. But it doesn't work. The enormity is inconceivable. I learned more by painting this globe during just a few evenings than all my studies in school.

I touched my tiny brush onto Europe—I had less than a few seconds to visit the complex histories, the glorious art and architecture, the many languages/cultures/traditions, the past dynamic of royalty and peasantry, the countries whose peoples had invaded and massacred one another for centuries. As the whiteness claimed the boundaries and names, I watched the whole region blend into a union. Ah, now I see: look at this oh-so-tiny landmass which has been the scene of such history!

I touched my brush to places in the Arctic—some named for a brave adventurer who had gruesomely staked his life on the discovery, some named for a Prince or Queen whose pride and importance were once of such consequence but who now are utterly unknown and unimportant.

I touched my brush to the great continent of Africa—aware of the ruinous history of brutal colonialism, resulting in its current state of unspeakable warfare, poverty, disease, and hunger for nearly a billion people.

I touched my brush to the coastlines of the world, knowing that over 50% of the world population is located on the coastlines, knowing the increasing hordes of people crowded into those spaces devouring fish and land.

I touched my brush to the vast expanses of land uninhabitable to people—the arid, scorching Sahara Desert; the barren, freezing wastelands of the Siberian Plains; the incomparably frozen, sub-zero world of Antarctica—knowing full well that hospitality to people is not a criteria for beauty, meaning, or importance of landforms.

Everywhere I touched my brush, there was the history of that place, a story of people there now, a vision of the natural world now and before, a realization that *this place is here, now, for real.*

There were recent events—the earthquake in Turkey, the refugees in Kosovo, the turmoil in East Timor…There were past events— the Roman empire, the era of African slave trade, the holocaust of Nazi Germany, the Renaissance, the Egyptian empire…There were the far distant events—the slamming of the Indian subcontinent into Asia causing the upheaval of the Himalayas, the splitting of South America and Africa, the ebb and flow of the Ice Ages. There were the natural worlds of Life, and Life's recent encounter and alteration with the onslaught of human population. Everywhere I touched, so much to understand, to see, to consider about the Earth, time, humanity.

I touched my brush to the oceans—once the coastline details were outlined and the smaller areas defined, I used a large, *three-inch* wide brush. Ocean upon ocean upon ocean. Planet Water. So much water. Intellectually, we all know about it. Yeah, yeah, yeah, the planet is covered over 70% by water (include the ice and we land-lubbers might get 15%; include those uninhabitable deserts and we're down to 10% of the world for us. We currently occupy only 4% of the planet!) But no one really believes this or sees it. If we do, it explodes all of our myths and concepts. It compromises our sovereignty. It reduces our almighty stature to overwhelming in-significance. We dare not look.

Ultimately, we dare not look upon reality as it is. This, it seems, is our creed.

Now, I have painted a globe.

It looked so strange and unfamiliar once it was stripped of all the human distinctions and the water was all blue and the land all colored as it might be seen from space. With no human words to designate the nations, the cities, the mountains, rivers, oceans, currents, ocean trenches, longitudes/latitudes, equator/polar circles—with all of that removed, it looked so simple, so plain, so stark. The landforms looked somehow as if they had shrunk. The whole globe was so obviously dominated by water. Without all the distracting hubbub, the Pacific Ocean finally appeared in its reality: covering fully half of the planet! Asia looked so huge. Africa looked so dry, the United States looked so insignificant, and all nationality was dissolved.

These specific comments are also and always so dramatically attested to by those who have actually seen the planet from space. Of course, those space traveller's experience of *actuality*—witnessing the glorious three-dimensional sphere against the ever-so-real backdrop of unfathomable blackness—is understandably life-changing. But even I was surprised by the impact this simply painted globe had on me.

It didn't happen until I had begun the process of overlaying the cloud system over the land and water. Throughout this painting, I have utilized photographs taken from space in order to maintain a factual depiction. I have painted this globe with the diligence of an 18th century portraitist. Though I shirk at the inadequacy of my skill in depicting this grand orb, nevertheless I strove for accuracy to the best of my ability. In this, it should be noted, I saw how inaccurate most satellite depictions actually are. One glaring error is that they depict large landform areas as green. Anyone who has looked at photos from space, even photos which are color enhanced, can observe: nothing on Earth appears green, even the lushest, greenest areas. The effects of atmospheric reflection cause such areas to appear dark blue. This can even be seen on Earth when looking at verdant hillsides from a distance of twenty miles. They don't look green. The other error usually made is clearly in view of the usual reason people buy a globe: they want to see things about the *land* on Earth, i.e. they are not interested in the 40-60% cloud cover that is always hanging around the planet. We *expect* cloudlessness with the usual worded globes—but a view from space! Even in actual satellite images, they manage to reduce cloud cover to a politically correct, intellectually acceptable 10% or so. It looks so naked.

I used photos of various views of the Earth to accurately paint the cloud cover. Again, I learned so much: how *white* clouds are; how clouds bump into coastlines and continents; how they swirl with the Earth's rotation; how the equatorial cloud belt wraps around the Earth; how at the poles the land, ice, and clouds appear indistinguishable from one another...

But somewhere along the way of dabbing that whiteness to duplicate those swirls and blotches, the illusion of the actual Earth came into my view, and something happened to me.

At the time, I wrote: "Suddenly with this, I feel utter awe with what this is. I am stunned, sickened even—it affects me so. I break to be stunned and finally decide, I really cannot do any more tonight."

To see the Earth from space is one of the most significant accomplishments of humankind. I recently read a quote from Socrates (fully 2,500 years ago!), saying that if we could just see this, humanity would be lifted up to true consciousness. Unfortunately, it hasn't worked. Remarkable photographs of the Earth from space have become so familiar and commercially overused in this era as to now appear trite and hackneyed. It is interesting to note, however, that we only seem to have embraced this image in *two-dimensions*. The biggest globe makers have at least once (and I think even twice) thought that people would be interested in a three-dimensional image of the Earth from space, but found too few customers to warrant continuation.

I conjecture that we are not ready. Although we are technologically capable of seeing the actual Earth from space, we are not yet psychologically/psychically ready to truly see the Earth as a three-dimensional sphere. We—specifically the *technologically advanced* humans—are fundamentally two-dimension oriented and are becoming increasingly more, not less, two-dimensional in our thinking, our seeing, and our activities. We invest more and still more into the development and focus of two-dimensionality.

Yet the Earth is a globe...a sphere. Every depiction of it in two-dimensions is a distortion. To really see the Earth, we must see it spherically.

We huddle around our globes as they are, endless fonts of human-designated information. We cling to our words, our distinctions, our categories and definitions. We have named everything now, and whatever else there is to be found, we will name that too. This is all well and good.

But we will never really see or understand where and who we are until we drop our human-created distinctions and observe what actually is. If we are only self-referential, how can we perceive the enormity of all that which is not us?

September 1999

~

We Call This *Progress*?

We have figured out how to lift tons into the air and
       fly around the world in hours.
We have figured out how to travel the vast and deep oceans in days.
We can now talk with each other anywhere on the planet.
And calculate untold amounts of information.

But we have not yet figured out
How to stop doing cruel and horrid things to one another.

We have figured out how to make an acre of land
Yield food that before took one hundred acres.
We have invented a crop of corn that can endure drought.
We have figured out how to *make* a pig or chicken grow meaty in months.
And how to clone a sheep.

But we have not yet figured out
How to keep all our children fed and healthy.

We have machines to do the labor of millions of workers.
We have technologies to move us, think for us,
       protect us, educate us, communicate for us.

But we have not yet learned
How to end poverty, oppression, slavery, nor hatred.

We have provided many with luxuries and conveniences.
We have amassed vast empires of wealth for a few.
But we have disconnected ourselves from the essentials of life itself,
While leaving billions without the barest necessities.

We have flung our machines into the heavens.
We have encroached upon and affected
Every domain of all other Earth creatures.
We have proliferated our bodies, our cultures,
        our beliefs, our human-created dimensions.

But we have not yet found
A way to live in reverence of the infinite miracle of simply being.
We have not yet found a way to live in peace, being human.

February 1999

~

TITANIC AS METAPHOR

Horrendously and unbelievably, it cost $225 million to create the film of the year, *Titanic*. Reprehensible as that may be—as well as flawed with triteness, flat romanticism, and a variety of hokey contrivances—nevertheless it has won people, young and old; it has won a variety of film awards; it has far outgrossed its expenses; and it has rekindled the never-dying fascination with this tiny, dramatic tragedy. It has even revived the decades-old question of *why*? Why does this story so captivate people?

In so many ways it is a microcosm of life, examined under the looking glass of heightened drama. As I watched it recently, I saw it as a disturbingly apt metaphor for our current times.

The idea that we are currently entering an era where starvation, disease, poverty, overpopulation, climatic change, and resource depletion are about to become widespread realities seems to most people (especially Americans) as unfounded and absurd as the thought that the Titanic was even remotely sinkable. Our obliviousness to this as a possibility has blind-sighted us to indications to the contrary. Our ill-preparedness for such tragedy is comparable to the shortfall of lifeboats on the Titanic—sinking was so unthinkable, it was a mere formality to have lifeboats and seemed quite understandable to not bother having enough for all passengers. Such is our confidence in the power of our technologies, human ingenuity, and sheer adaptability—we have no strategic plan for dealing with worldwide crisis. In Titanic retrospection, it is easy to piece together the collection of critical nodal points, some even quite minor (such as the lack of binoculars for the crow's nest lookout), any one of which might have resulted in a less disastrous conclusion. What are the minor oversights in our current situations which in retrospect will appear as such glaring errors of judgment? Twenty years from now, might we see our lack of action in the 1990's to shift dramatically and immediately to non-polluting fuels as foolish as launching a ship with less than half the lifeboats needed?

The brutally explicit stratification of classes by economic status on the Titanic—including not only differences in accommodations and decks, but also in entertainment, food, personnel, china...in short everything—is no different than the current global inequities. Although the term *Third World*—with its close kinship to the term *third class*—has been unofficially banished as politically incorrect, we have now substituted *less developed* as the currently in-vogue alternative, for some distinction of this sort is simply a necessity in the presentation and compilation of global information. Just as on the Titanic, where the survival statistics correlate specifically to the status of the people, the same is true in our world today; whether we are compiling facts about mortality, economics, population growth, literacy, health, and so on—the information clearly splits itself by similarities into two categories, and however we choose to call them, it is quite basically, the *haves* and the *have-nots*, to varying degrees.

With righteous disdain we have catalogued how selfishly and connivingly the wealthy aboard the Titanic maneuvered themselves into the lifeboats, even launching those precious few boats with twelve or twenty aboard instead of seventy! And then we observe in the movie the harrowing reality of people safe in their lifeboats, just one-quarter mile from the ship, as they listened to hundreds of people plunged into the icy water, screaming for help, drowning to death. Only one boat went back to help them, recovering only six people! But is this any different than our own self-serving indifference to the devastating suffering of people capsizing by the millions, even *billions*, in the *less developed* nations?

April 1998

$\backsim$

WE ARE A WORLD GONE MAD

When I woke up at 2:00 a.m. this morning and was quite wakeful, I began to read the latest issue of World Watch (March/April 1998). I read it through cover to cover. Half-way through, I was in tears—overwhelmed with the disastrous impacts and conditions of the human-created world. We are a world gone mad, I realized.

I read the editorials and letters. The articles and summaries. But as I read, there were also the million thoughts and understandings beyond what was said that trickled through my mind. It was a shocking inundation, beginning on the first page with the manipulative and deceptive degradation of the USDA standards for *organic* foods in order to capitalize on the growing market for such foods. And then: a letter discussing the ludicrous impropriety of the new environmentalists' practice of putting an economic price tag on *nature's services*, in order to bring awareness of the value of the environment. Letters about the relationship of population to climate change. A bullshit political statement letter (I am sorry to characterize it such, but it really was) from Al Gore, Vice President of the USA, regarding the Kyoto Conference and the administration's commitment to a "cleaner earth." The use of hazardous irradiation processes on meats in attempts to protect people from the deadly bacteria of factory farming. News about the spread of HIV/AIDS (more than 1,000 children infected every *day*, 90% in sub-Saharan Africa; 500 US children infected in a year). Forest fires raging around the world. Deforestation occurring as coffee growers turn to higher yield, suntolerant varieties. And all this was only by page nine! Then a main article about fish farming, (which did not mention the devastating decline of nearly every oceanic fishery on the globe) examining in detail the problems fish farming is causing in land erosion, fish disease, water pollution, displacement of people and cultures, overfishing for *fish meal* to feed the farmed fish, and more. "Paper Forests," a detailed article about the billions of trees planted in unsustainable circumstances trying "to meet the world's soaring appetite for paper." An article which traced the making of a pair of athletic shoes, complete with its responsibility for the exploitation of poverty-stricken people the world over with hazardous pollutants carelessly created all the while. A discussion of the Kyoto Climate Treaty, barely glancing over one representative outrage: *buying* and *selling* emissions *credits* to meet criteria! The final page photo of the enormous electric towers in Canada, drooped and crumbled under the weight of the ice storm, was paired with fitting poetry: *"Some say the world will end in fire; Some say in ice. —Robert Frost."*

Too many. There are simply too many of us. At this point, there is almost nothing we can do to steer clear of the disasters we are headed towards. Anything we are doing and have done would work on a small scale. At the scale of demand we are operating at, whether it is in terms of paper, lumber, fish, grain, coffee, athletic shoes, organic produce—whatever it is, simply because of the enormity of scale, it has become unsustainable. The Western world has enslaved the Asian world, a trend which will continue only until the Western empire has fallen and the Asian, especially China, takes precedence. The African world is being left to self-immolate in drought, starvation, disease, poverty, and violence. South America is scrambling to compete for enslavement but has lost. We speak of the manufacture, processing, ecological impacts, economic viability, sustainability, and future yields of living beings—plants, trees, fish, cows, chickens, shrimp—as if they were inanimate assembly-line units intended to serve the needs of humans, if only we can be clever enough to figure how to best manipulate them to fulfill that purpose, hopefully without destroying our world.

We are a world gone mad and there is no turning back. It is not that virtue, compassion, spirituality, and wisdom are dead. All of that is as alive in its minority and/or silence as it has been at any time prior. Unfortunately however, and historically, true spiritual rectitude has *never* afforded *any* people immunity from annihilation. Our world historically has been, and continues to be, dictated, that is ruled, by ignorance (simple, even innocent, unknowing/unawareness), inertia (the tendency to simply continue in the same direction), greed, and cruelty. Our sheer numbers, our technological *advances*, and our global interconnectedness has now rendered such dictators fatal.

I listen to my friends and peers grapple with their personal trials and triumphs the same way I listen to children—with love, patience, and respect for their experience of reality, and yet from a perspective utterly beyond their comprehension.

I continue my everyday life of comfort, security, luxury, freedom as if in a surrealistic dream, ever aware not only of that expanded view of our world and times, but too of my own greed, hypocrisy, complacency, shame, and complicity.

It would be hard to look upon us in impartial judgment and not conclude: We, the human race, are a plight and shame on our Earth. We have been incorrigibly irresponsible with sacred Life on this exquisite gem in the Universe. In this one aspect alone we are perhaps so guilty and sinful, there can be no absolution. We have ruthlessly plundered, mutilated, murdered, exploited, demeaned, enslaved, disfigured, manipulated, and exterminated not only those of our *own* family, but of every family of Life on the planet that we possibly could. For this alone, I stand before my world each day and helplessly cry out, "Forgive us, for we know not what we do." Seen in its truth and magnitude, it is simply unpardonable. Even sadder, it is unstoppable.

We are a world gone mad.

March 1998

~

The Earthscape Paintings At The Salt Monument

I fall to the floor weeping before these canvases—reduced to cheap mediocrity in my every attempt to do justice to this magnificent vision.

This view! Although I have never actually witnessed the reality of this planet seen from two hundred miles above, I have on occasion been briefly shocked in that vision by intensively steeping myself in the photographs and words of those who have. Just as there are realms of consciousness that can only be known in direct experience—no description, however accurate or genuine, can ever convey it—so is the actual view of Earth from space. There is nothing else like it. There is nothing in our human view that allows it. As such, our usual response to these images is that we simply do not *see* them—not really. We look, but our seeing is flat, two-dimensional, blasé, superficial—unaccepting, inured to the profound, mystical reality.

This color! How far I am from even barely depicting its subtlety and perplexity; how frustratingly incapable of crafting my palette to bear resemblance to the actuality. I try and try again and fall short and then still shorter. What is that incomparable shading of this desert? What is that elusive violet haze towards the horizon? What colors could combine to create the exquisite, incomprehensible blueness of this sea which is not just *blue* but rather a fathomless concoction of vivid nuance.

This complexity! In one sweeping view of a continent: A billion people, of whom scarcely a trace can be detected! Millions of miles of forests! Vast regions teeming with life! And all of us virtually invisible, utterly, undeniably insignificant. The details of mountain folds and river courses, shorelines and deserts—*details*! But what here appears as details are actually forms that are hundreds, even thousands, of miles large.

Oh, how pathetically short my words fall as well. I am as incapable of bringing what I see/feel/experience into words as I am unable to depict it in painting. I am overcome with frustration, perturbation, inadequacy. I even yearn to be released from the mandate to create this series; how can I even minimally perform the honor that is due? The incomprehensible, (ironically) *other-worldly* beauty of this planet seen from a distance! The complex and crucial philosophical import this view wordlessly, silently conveys!

Nearly every one of the 350-400 people who have witnessed Earth from orbit has been profoundly and irreversibly changed. When we truly see where we are, unforgettable awe is the only response. However, their photographs and exclamations apparently have hardly impacted the remaining billions of us.

It was fully twelve years ago that I first conceived the Earthscape series. I saw then: no artist has adopted this subject matter as their genre! I was so surprised; it seems like such an obvious subject matter. I thought then, even in terms of popular art: wouldn't people love a painting of their homeland or favorite place as seen from the unique, mind-expanding view from space? I saw it as a whole new art form! Is it possible that even now, twelve years later, there is *still* no one who has engaged in this as an art form?! (I am at least aware of no one.) This is parallel to the absence for centuries in European art of a whole variety of subjects which eventually became commonplace: landscape! How unimaginable it is but this was never the *subject* of any European painting for hundreds upon hundreds of years!; neither were scenes from every day life. It is hard to believe that it wasn't until the end of the 1800's that such subjects were received in art circles.

However, even despite my initial enthusiasm in the late 1980's, I did nothing until now. Perhaps I lacked the time and focus then, but even now, I would have this cup pass if I felt I could. I confess here: not only do I lack the courage and competency to do this series, I don't even *like* the idea of all these proposed paintings hanging in the current room of the Salt Monument! And yet, it is the room itself, the "empty" upper walls, (and perhaps the Salt Monument, itself) that called forth these paintings. I go on record: it is truly despite myself that I go forward in this massive, bothersome, confronting series.

Thankfully after a few weeks of seeking and waiting, I did finally figure out the musical accompaniment for these paintings—in such painting works, I often find a passionate fellowship in one particular musical piece. Who should show up but Mozart, with a chorale no less!? I cannot really imagine that the less-than-seven-minute *Kyrie* of the *Great Mass in C minor* (KV 427) will hold through this entire fifteen-plus projected painting series, but for now, I simply cannot hear it enough. Most specifically, the sweeping surge that so ungraspably bursts within the very first two minutes from a quiescent, introductory lilt into blazing, impassioned ecstasy—ah! Somehow *this* is the ideal companion to my overwhelmed wonder of the true majesty these paintings signify. A month later, my listening expanded to include almost the entire Mass. To my ecstasy, I found an even *more* extraordinary swell in the first thirty seconds of the *Jesu Christe* segment of the *Gloria* section. In this—in what is perhaps the most ultimately beautiful musical moment of all time, the epitome of what is most perfect and divine—I have myself been physically transported into space to witness the *actual reality* of the sight of the Earth from space. Streaming with tears, in absolute awe, this musical sequence has given me the true experience that these paintings merely, and so inadequately, hint at. My hope is only that somehow the transference of these mystically charged moments are infused within the paintings themselves for the viewer.

Ah, but even with all *these* words, I have left entirely unmentioned my two very favorite parts of these images! First, the mesmerizing black void beyond the horizon of Earth, the ever-consistent backdrop to the Earth—with what passion I slather the blackest of blackness upon these sections, drinking in its paradoxical brilliance and inscrutable depth. There will never be enough words to express what this is nor how much I love it. Secondly, the "ever-so-thin day-blue veil of our atmosphere" [quoted from the Daily Ceremony at the Salt Monument]. The depiction of this tiny seam of iridescence—the very hem of life on Earth; that frighteningly scant border between all to which we are bound in *familiarity* (i.e. of the one family of Earth) and the inhospitable, vast blackness—ah! Forever ineffable and unportrayable. So sacred…so mystical…so elusive.

October 2001

~

Four Immediate Problems Facing Humanity

They are seemingly unrelated, and yet quite interconnected. They are largely invisible and unnoticed, but deadly. Any one by itself might cause some problems, but all of them together spell disaster. With one exception, they could all be shifted into constructive trends within a period of ten years, but that type of shift would represent such an enormous revolution of thought and action, it is not reasonable to even consider such a radical response (short of some truly dramatic, highly unlikely, short term cataclysmic event, i.e. polar shift, asteroid to hit Earth, etc.).

How can one summarize the principal problems currently facing humanity in four simple headings?

Economics, the global dictator. As I have written elsewhere, this is the most dangerous, insidious, and completely unrecognized problem of our world. I realize that my view of this is largely utterly incomprehensible to others, yet there is nothing of which I am more certain. The globalization of money as the determinant of value, action, meaning, relationship, lifestyle, et al, has become an invisible problem of such proportion it seems virtually incorrectable. I still maintain that a global revolution of virtue and inner worth could possibly occur, even it if is perhaps inspired by a devastating economic collapse.

Population. The single gravest and most determining factor of our future is linked to our enormous population. Human activities, industries, and even simple needs (i.e. water, shelter, food) which might be fairly harmless in small doses, have and will become increasingly threatening simply by the increase in scale. A few billion people needing food over a few hundred years is very different than six to eight billion people needing food every year over thirty years. Because of the gradual and seemingly imperceptible growth of human population and all its impacts, the significance of our population to our future is almost entirely overlooked. No one is really dealing with this concern at the level it needs to be considered. Population planning on a global scale is still considered highly controversial, although the population issue has gained considerable visibility and is generally, though vaguely, considered a major concern. Yet even family planning at a global level of massive reform to reduce the growth rates to absolute goals will not address the unprecedented increase of another three billion people in the next fifty years. This is the unspoken issue. Of the four problems listed here, this is the only one that cannot be shifted by radical action within a ten year period. Our population growth, by the very nature of its current momentum, cannot be halted yet, even if there were complete intention, action, and cooperation.

Fossil fuels/toxins. The damaging effects of the widespread and ever increasing use of fossil fuels has certainly become more publicized and debated during the past fifteen years. Yet as we can witness by the recent conference in Kyoto, energetic reform towards nonpolluting, renewable sources of energy is still a long way off. Powerfully connected to the economic dictator, the short-lived fossil fuel industry (doomed by finiteness to end within fifty to seventy years), currently dominates the global economy and military action. Nothing has yet proven itself more powerful, not even the sincere pleas of scientific knowledge declaring that the very earth systems upon which we are utterly dependent are truly endangered by continuing usage of fossil fuels. A radical and rapid shift to other preferable energy sources is definitely feasible, but can only be successful if linked advantageously into the economic dictatorship. All other human-industry-created toxins—whose destructive properties we know and also do not—which we are dumping into our air, atmosphere, soil, and water in ever larger quantities are also included in this problem.

Livestock products. Of these four problems, this is probably the least understood, most overlooked, most easily changed, and most underestimated. Few people have any inkling that this is a major, serious, immediate problem facing humanity. The increasing use of what is euphemistically and so clinically referred to as "livestock products" (i.e. cows, pigs, chickens, fish, dairy, eggs, etc.) for human consumption is the single greatest contributor to water shortage, soil destruction, loss of farmland, human hunger, and human illness. Additionally, it also surprisingly contributes considerably to water and atmospheric pollution, as well as human poverty. Yet we are witnessing an unbridled and completely ignorant trend of sharp increases in human diets shifting higher up the foood chain. Notably for example, the shift towards a diet of livestock products among the one billion people of China may represent the single most dangerous contributor to food scarcity in history—and yet the world as a whole remains utterly oblivious to this simple, provable concern. Again, a program of radical reform could effectively stem this problem in a relatively short period of time. Vegetarianism, promoted as a global practice, could benefit human health, longevity, economy, and ecology—yet resistance to such a reform, due to cultural, gastronomical, and economic forces is formidable and perhaps undefeatable.

The gravity of our problems cannot be underestimated. There are many other problems that are serious and in dire need of reform—for example, the rapid unprecedented destruction of an enormous number of species of life which will dramatically impact human agriculture and health over the next twenty years and cataclysmically affect the whole planet in the geologic timeframe; or the global war machine, which has $600 billion *annually* tied up in destructive and otherwise useless weaponry and toxic substances; and so on. Yet the four mentioned here are perhaps the most immediately pressing and hold the greatest potential for both disaster and reform.

With best wishes and love to humankind in facing our problems,

One human being.

April 1998

~

TRAGEDY: JOHN KENNEDY JR.

On days like this, the Salt Monument takes on a particularly ironic and profound note.

Today, Kennedy, his wife, and her sister died in an airplane crash. Television is brimming with the news, dramatizing the tragedy. People everywhere are stunned, reminded of the ever-so-thin veil between living and dying, the vulnerability we all share in this, the suffering of life embodied in this tragedy-ridden family. Here were people who epitomize most of the world's definition of all the best in life: fame, fortune, youth, beauty, intelligence, opportunity. Gone. Just like that: gone. None of those envied attributes can prevent unexpected death.

On days like this, the Salt Monument seems particularly profound. Today over 148,000 people died just like they do every day. To-day, I attended a memorial service for each of them to honor their heroic journey in life, as I do every day. Today, I mourned with their families, grieving the painful loss of a loved one, as I do every day. But today, many people are grappling with the death of these three.

Today, I took three grains of salt to represent these three people whose deaths are being observed by millions of people today. It is hard to select out just three grains of salt from the rest of the 148,000 grains whose destination is dissolution in the bowl of water today. I honored those three, along with the millions of other people hon-oring them today. And then there were the rest of the 148,000 people who died within this same twenty-four-hour period. Around the world, ten thousand and more other young adults were tragically killed today in accidents, in warfare, in disease—each one leaving an unerasable legacy of loss, grief, tragedy for their survivors. Today, as every day too, 33,000 young children actually died from poverty and malnourishment. 33,000. How can this be conceived, *every day*?

The perspective, poignancy, equanimity of the Salt Monument at such times is inexpressible. Nothing needs to be said at the Salt Monument. It just is and thus says it all.

I do also notice how in a world of global news, the death of no-tables/celebrities as well as the grievous tragedies (i.e. a commercial airline crash, a hurricane, a terrorist incident) has become the domain of all people. This is actually the second day like this at the Salt Monument. The first occurred with the Columbine High School shooting. (Another day like this *would* have been at the death of Princess Diana or the bombings in Kenya/Tanzania, but those occurred just prior to the beginning of the daily world births and deaths at the Salt Monument.) Everyone grieves these things via the news, and we do it together as such. This is why we need and are ready for the Salt Monument—it would be good to have a way to honor our grief, together and in perspective.

Certainly the Salt Monument's perspective is daunting, and this may ultimately be difficult for many. But it is a perspective that is entirely real: Yes, these three people died and it has our attention, but viewed in the context of the whole, we are confronted with the syzygy of significant/insignificant, one/many, meaning/meaninglessness. Death, perspective, time, cycles, reality are not to be understood easily.

One days like this, I am glad to have already been doing this every day.

July 1999

(Im)personal Dedication

At my daily bell meditation walk of gratitude,
I stood before the altar and bowed:

I am deeply grateful, honored, and humbled
to be entrusted with the Salt Monument.
I will do my best in every way to fulfill this mission.

September 1997

~

Always At The Salt Monument

The meaning, feeling, and awareness of the Salt Monument
Has become so imbedded in my being,
I realized recently: I am always at the Salt Monument.
Wherever I am, whatever I am doing,
Whatever I am thinking, whoever I am listening to,
All of it always is also at the Salt Monument.
It will not matter where I go from here;
The Salt Monument will forever go with me.

October 1999

~

I WILL DO MY BEST TO ACCEPT YOU

As the guardian of this body of humanity,
I will do my best to accept you—
Whether I pass you in my car,
Meet you as a friend,
Or never have an idea of who or where you are.

I will do my best to accept you fully,
To recognize your utter uniqueness
And too, acknowledge your similarity to me and everyone.

I will do my best to accept you
Whatever you are doing.
If you are cruel or oppressed,
If you are pure or vile,
If you are…whatever.

For me, here at this Monument,
You are here—
An actual crystal of your body is here in my present,
So I do my best to honor you.

October 1999

I Can Keep Silent No Longer: I *Have* A Hammer

Bursting from within me is a depth of love, joy, and knowledge that is so encompassing, I can no longer keep silent. I cannot *not* speak for peace. I cannot *not* speak day and night about our oneness as a family, the glory of our being on Earth, the preciousness of Life, the vastness of our Universe. Suddenly, with that thought, a song I haven't thought of for years burst forth from my heart. I *do* have a hammer and a bell! It's the bell and the hammer of the Salt Monument.

"If I had a hammer, I'd hammer in the morning. I'd hammer in the evening, all over this land. It's the hammer of justice. It's the hammer of freedom. It's the hammer of the love between my brothers and my sisters, all over this land. If I had a bell…If I had a song…"

At the Salt Monument we will meet soul to soul, human to human, as one grain of salt to another in the symbolic presence of all humanity as our witness. Here the leaders of the world—those to whom we have entrusted power and influence over our lives and our planet—will be invited to consider their actions and impacts from a deepened perspective. This is the ultimate purpose of the Salt Monument: to affect our world from the heart.

December 1997

~

I Am Only One Person

I am only one person.
Sincere in my heart,
I am overwhelmed by all the suffering I see.

Sincere in my heart,
I pray for the freedom of all.

But I am only one person.
I have no way to affect this.
My prayers are futile and powerless.
My tears do nothing to assuage the cruelties and injustice.

I am only one person,
Helplessly, hopelessly, but sincerely
Offering up a prayer of freedom for all of us.

February 1999

~

PASSION, PASSION, PASSION

To bring passion to every encounter, whether with ant or person, with rock or car—to love so intently, so completely, it explodes and annihilates. This is my work, my life, my expression.

This is why the Salt Monument as daily practice is so penetrating. To truly work each day to love *every* person, to honor each, remember each, to love each.

To be real about suffering—to awaken to it, feel it, weep it, see it!

Today I saw: I must continue to be who I am without any concern for fellowship, social acceptance, or recognition. I must go further, ever further, onward and onward in this intensity which compels and completes me. I cannot wait for others. I cannot consider the implications. I must be and be and be. My one hope in life is that I may perhaps in my lifetime meet one person with whom I can share and pass along all. (I have often thought this, and today was reminded of it in hearing about Sham-e Tabriz's similar wish being fulfilled in meeting Rumi—who took the sacred passion and knowledge into his own self and transmuted it forever.)

August 1999

~

Swallowed In A Sea of Prayers

I am witnessing a steady, foreseeable transformation of my life.
I am gradually and willingly being swallowed up in a sea of prayers.
More and more hours every day are being claimed
By my various dedications, practices, meditations…
More and more my life is pivoted on
How to complete all these in any given day.
It is my mainstay, my purpose, my focus.
There is little else I choose to do, have time to do, am interested to do.

July 1999

~

I SAT THERE AND ATE…

I sat down to eat yesterday. I didn't *need* to eat anything, and I was well aware of that. I had already eaten enough for the day.

I applied full awareness of what I was eating, a remarkable practice (in which we all *rarely* engage). I considered where each food had come from, how and where it had been grown, who had been involved in planting and harvesting it, how it got to me. This included how the wheat became flour became a tortilla; how the cows whose milk became the cheese had lived in conditions of torment, disease, pain; I saw their infected udders, and the antibiotics and drugs pumped into them; I smelled the stench of the manure-filled stalls. I witnessed how the olives had gotten into that can I had opened.

I sat there and ate in silence and awareness. In part I was sickened as I considered it, and also I continued to eat and enjoy my tasty meal.

I sat there and ate and placed myself in the dawning day that was at the moment occurring in Eritrea—a place considered by many as the most forsaken country on earth. I sat myself somewhere in that impoverished place, with my plate and my full stomach, eating my savory meal while people whose arms and legs more closely resembled twigs and branches gathered around and watched me eat my single unnecessary meal of more food than they had eaten in a month. Feeling like a selfish and gross glutton, I continued to eat.

I sat there and ate and became aware of all the insects who had been killed in the process of this food becoming my meal, of the poisoning of the air, the degradation of water...I realized that my cozy Chinese silk pajama pants were the result of the brutal death of thousands of caterpillars—how can *I* even wear silk!?

What *can* we do that does not contribute to the destruction of other forms of life, to the degeneration of our Earth, to the exploitation of other people? The Jains have taken that level of awareness to the very extreme of action, and yet admittedly even their meticulous care is ultimately futile and intensely unnatural. How can we bear to truly be aware?

I sat there and ate.

July 1999

~

I Cry, and Do Nothing

There is no glory in this duty of mine (the daily Salt Monument ceremony). It is even so senseless and ineffectual, I could feel ashamed of it. I could also perhaps feel proud of it. But I do not feel either. Everyone has a job of some sort. This is mine. In the scheme of things, it clearly means nothing.

I watched 30,000 children die today. I did nothing but cry. I saw many people hacked to death and other sheer cruelties. I did nothing but cry. I heard tens of thousands of people dying from hunger and disease. I did nothing but cry.

This all happens every day and again. I cry, and do nothing.

October 1999

~

An Evening At The Salt Monument

I do not rush to fulfill my duty at the Salt Monument each day. It is neither comfortable nor easy to stretch myself into the disquieting reality that there really are six billion others just as self-absorbed as I in their own lives. But this is not the only thing I force myself to do each day. Neither do I hasten to stretch myself daily in my Yoga practice—who hurries to turn oneself into a pretzel or to be reminded of how unconscious and unconscionable we are with our sacred, magical bodily vessel? Neither do I race to fulfill the daily *Earth cycle prayers*, by which I impel myself to expand to the actuality of this huge spherical planet, to visit all its regions and places, to witness the true cast of life characters, and to observe our true placement in the solar system/galaxy/universe. Neither do I rush to enact my daily bell walk of gratitude. Who really wants to face their every completely-taken-for-granted wholly undeserved privilege in stark contrast to the woeful, undeserved disadvantage of so many others?

These duties I fulfill might better be seen as something akin to the Sundance ceremony of native Indians. It is duty, honor, transcendent, deeply teaching—but it can hardly be called fun or entertainment. It involves pain, surrender, concentration, dedication. I do these things because I know I am better for it. Without these practices, my life would be empty, my self consumed by egoic absorption, my perspective skewed and ever-so-local.

During the summer schedule here, it is often two (and even later) in the morning, that I finally drag myself out to the Salt Monument, tired and self-absorbed, unable to imagine that I can offer the necessary obeisance to each and every person, and especially to those (the newborn and just dead) for whom this day was actually so intensely special and very real. I walk into the Monument's room to step into my function and from knowing/feeling/thinking nothing, I am swept into a tornado.

What follows are my notes from *one* evening experience at the Salt Monument:

 ~ Sitting contemplation: there really are this many. I still can never believe it.

 ~ Song with harp: "Take my hand, let us walk through the Valley of Death," with the children who died today.

 ~ Deaths: Great weeping. First I die today, then all my loved ones, and then the children. As an elderly person, watching all my friends dying.

 ~ Touching the births. Giving love to each, their purity and clear consciousness, blessing their journey, beginning their breathing with the rest of us breathing, joining the circling days with us.

 ~ People at their workings. An image montage of six billion people engaged in their labors: the vast corps of all those in the world engaged in growing/gathering/ transporting/preparing/packaging/etc. food for us, the students learning us, mothers caring for us, warriors protecting us, politicians governing us, scientists discovering us...and...

 ~ Prayer to those filled with hatred today; going back with them to their original state of purity and innocence at birth, mourning the unnatural injury that brought them to this hatred today.

 ~ Intense encounter of openness to what the Salt Monument is; simple pure face-to-face empty/filled. I let all go and open completely, I am flooded with sacredness beyond all. Tears just flowed like a mountain river.

That was during one session. What can I say? It's intense.

And it happens day after day after day—not every day, but almost. The following are notes from experiences at the Salt Monument on *other* days, all just during *this week*.

~ Prayer of love and thanks to all those in the world who were kind today.

~ I was so tired, the harp song connects me with all those in the world who are *really* tired today.

~ Deaths: celebrating for each who died today—no more hunger, toil, pain, illness, suffering.

~ Births: we have each had a *first* day.

~ Prayer to those who are marginalized, discriminated against…

~ Song: image of the Earth passage through our space circle— one year and all the activities in the circling circles.

~ Deaths: realization about passing through—we are all just passing through; the divine senselessness of life.

~ For the first time I lie down *under* the Salt Monument— amazing: one ton suspended over my body…all the people. I experience this as the place/way I would like to die, my death in the future…what a way to go! I see everything about who I am and what I am doing as never before. Oh words so inadequate. Awareness at my death of all the others who are dying too that day and also, as I die, aware of all the births on that day.

~ I cannot remember it now, but the post-deaths/births contemplation was *searingly* profound tonight. This divine life is endlessly rich.

~ Song: bringing to the presence of the Salt Monument all the truly great human beings, past and present…the ones we know were/are truly great. All gathered at the Salt Monument because they all were/are here.

~ Births: time to start eating (of the Earth's *products*.)

~ Contemplation: what if the Salt Monument had been started *x* years ago…50, 100, 1000… Considering this brings awareness of how amazing it is.

August 1999

~

I INVENTED A TEACHER

There are those gracious few who come into the world and become a great teacher to humankind. Those best known and thus presumed to be the greatest of these are called Mohammed, Jesus, Buddha. Less aggrandized and recent were perhaps Gandhi, the Dalai Lama, Mother Theresa. For these people, their life itself is the embodiment of a teaching. After their death, their memory becomes a body of teaching, extending beyond time, place, individual. However, very few, if any, of these teachers were able to overcome or circumvent the essential problem in their teaching: people's attachment to the teacher's personality and individual identity.

We would feel amiss to call the earliest devotees of Jesus, Buddha, Mohammed cult followers but clearly this is true. And even more so, what they created and passed on to successive generations became ever increasingly more cultic. We call it religion. The religion that was created by the followers in the wake of these great teachers was not ever their teacher's intention or mission. The truth was: there was a person; the person was incredibly wise and enlightened; the person tried to teach others to be kind and happy; people loved this person; and that person died.

In this, perhaps only Lao Tzu escaped. Although a long-lived practice (Taoism) is based considerably on his teachings, he successfully prevented *Lao-tzuism* from becoming a religion or tradition. I believe he did this quite intentionally and consciously. He lived much of his life in the mainstream and yet relatively obscure, and then simply left the whole scene before anyone could form a cult around him. The book he left behind, *Tao De Ching*, said everything he wanted/needed to say. He removed his personality and thus no one was able to create a cult around it. I have always respected this. From the standpoint of the historical record, this is *very* difficult, or apparently near-impossible, to do—whether one is a greater or lesser teacher.

It suddenly occurred to me one day recently: I have *invented* a teacher! *I* am not the teacher (although I surely am a teacher and I can/do play that role). I am not inventing a teaching. Instead what I have done is to invent a great teacher itself: the Salt Monument. Of course this teacher is utterly sublime because this teacher is: ageless, wordless, immortal, wise, profound, subtle, universal, non-conceptual, and more. Most importantly, this teacher has no personality or identity which people will amplify. And whatever cult may form around the Salt Monument, I can see to it that it will not be based on the identity/personality of its inventor/creator, Margot Weiss. The Salt Monument is an independent, wholly impersonal teacher.

Of anything about my individual self having created the Salt Monument, it is this which I most celebrate: the Salt Monument has nothing to do with *me*.

September 1999

~

A Glimpse Of Agony

I have just completed today's Salt Monument prayers and ceremony.

Today's song—stimulated by the painful photograph of eight-year-old Omayra Sanchez, just prior to her drowning in an earthquake's flood...stimulated by hearing about the gruesome Pinochet regime of terror in Chile which reigned for over twenty years...stimulated by knowing what I know is happening all around the world in countless places—was the voices of several people around the world speaking to those of us who stand by watching: "Here we are dying of hunger, murdered by dictators, tortured in the name of hatred, and you are standing by, watching, watching this happen; sometimes you take photographs and report about it." It was so true and so painful, after a while I couldn't sing—my tears had drenched and choked me.

I went to sit for the deaths ceremony and I thought; oh no, not again. I must do this again. Another day of deaths. I began to weep before I even began. Not for death, but for the agony so many are living in. I felt it. Agony. I have wept before in the enormity of suffering, but today I experienced something I have never known: *agony*. The pain of torture, the suffering of violence, the fear of immanent cruelty, the grief of watching those we love suffer horribly...waves upon waves of it buffeted me. Tears hardly touched this grief. Instead I wailed. I sat there tonight at the Salt Monument and wailed loudly and unendingly. I wailed in utter agony. I became every person in a state of agony on this day. It was so painful, and there was no end. I could hardly bear it. Eventually, it subsided and I completed the deaths ceremony—ah, you are the fortunate ones: released, relieved, liberated. For them at least, the agony is over. And then I stood up to proceed. Time to love and bless the newborns…holding them to my heart, breathing their first breath with them, loving the pure being of each forever, welcoming them to this place.

I have let the whole world into my life, into my home, into my body. There is no turning back. I cannot stop. One could wonder if doing this might be dangerous to my health, physically or mentally. How could someone be committed to engage in a realistic awareness of all the people, all the births, all the deaths, all the feelings, all the all as much as humanly possible every day and not be personally endangered?! Oh, that concern is long past for me. My miniscule personal existence has long ago ceased to be of any significance here.

Yes, sometimes it does all seem more than I can bear. Not only the agony but the bliss as well. And then I go on to find still more and ever more that I have neglected or forgotten, been insensitive to and ignorant about, been superficial and unaware of. There is always another day and another. The moments of intense agony pass, the moments of intense joy pass. There is always another moment and another. I have now understood: it will be this way for the rest of my life.

October 1999

~

The Body Of Salt Was Seen Breathing!

It happened several weeks ago, and I now seem to have little else to say about this than just that. I was in meditation of the infants of our world, represented by the topmost layer of salt and the *birth cone*. I was deep in contemplation of these hundreds of millions of babies in all their life experiences of that moment. Surrealistically, I began to see the circular wave patterns on the surface body of salt slowly undulating in wave motion. My seeing of this was so evident, I realized it could be categorized as hallucination! Allowing that insanity, I nevertheless flowed with the vision to engage it fully. Breathing...I saw the body of humanity breathing!

November 1999

~

FEELING THE NEWS

So subtle, so vast, so…I watch the BBC World News, and instantly people from around the world are sitting in my house speaking the horrors and anger and futility they are living. Widows and mothers fighting against those who murdered their husbands and sons. The disasters of Kashmir, Palestine, South Africa, and more, shown in shining color—the self-created miseries of humans—against a backdrop of exquisitely beautiful jungles, forests, deserts, mountains, and meadows; amidst gentle, hardworking people who want only to live their simple lives without bloodshed and fear. Oh, I sit at the Salt Monument and cry out to us. We are so many, and so brutal, horrid, unspeakably horrible. Oh god, oh god.

November 2000

~

When Would *You* Do The Ceremony?!

"When do you do the ceremony?" people regularly and so casually ask, curious and practical.

Oh god. I could ask them: When would *you* do it? Imagine you knew that at some time during this day you were going to find out that your dearest loved one had just died. *And* that you were going to visit the woeful poverty of billions of people. *And* you were going to receive a full realization of your utter insignificance, vanity, and the general futility of your life and everyone else's. *And* you were going to look into the eyes of 30,000 young children just before they died all because they were too poor, even though you had promised to care for them. *And*, and and...

Well...when would *you* schedule to do all that (knowing you *had* to)?

It's hard, folks. It's hard to do this every day.

January 2001

~

I Opened My Eyes

I opened my eyes,
And I saw—

Flowers,
Trees,
Sunrise,
Murder,
Creatures,
And more creatures,
Horrors,
Tenderness,
Beauty,
Stars

I opened my eyes
And saw.

December 2000

ACKNOWLEDGEMENTS AND NOTES

∾ With special gratitude to Marcy Mae Mullet, for endlessly, dependably, and cheerfully typing all the text for this volume, and to Glenda Buchanan for her artful and exacting publishing skills in the design and typesetting of this book. Your assistance in producing this volume was invaluable.

∾ Special thanks to William Fraser Joseph Mullet—the first person in the world whose grain of salt was placed in the Salt Monument by a family member on his actual day of birth, August 12, 2002—whose handprint appears on the page for *Our Children* (page 119).

∾ Also special thanks to Rob, Merrin, and Brock Meltzer—whose hand tracings were utilized on *Radical Compassion* (page 75), and Marlee Meltzer whose hand print appears on *Songs at the Salt Monument* (page 97). The photograph of *The Monument Itself* (page 15) was taken by Tonya Goodwin on September 16, 2000. All other photographs and images are by Margot Weiss.

∾ The *One Hand* daily practice as described in *The Daily Ceremony* (page 13) is currently being observed every day by a handful of people in North America and Europe. The time selected for *Global Roll Call* each day is based on the greatest feasibility for the maximum number of people in the world. You are invited to join us by raising your hand---wherever you are, whatever the circumstances---for a moment of presence. This occurs at 2:00 pm UTC (Universal Time/Greenwich Mean Time) Standard Time, which is, for example, 7:00 am in Colorado, 9:00 am in New York, 4:00 pm in Sudan; 7:00 pm in Pakistan, 11:00 pm in Japan. Please note it is always at Standard Time (ST), not Daylight Savings Time (DST), so if/when your locale is observing DST you would adjust the time accordingly. (For example, during the summer in Colorado, *One Hand* is at 8:00 am.)

∽ All proceeds from this book will be dedicated to the perpetuation of the Salt Monument.

∽ At the juncture of the fifth anniversary, a permanent site where the Salt Monument will reside in perpetuity for all generations of humankind is being sought. If there is any way you can help found this Sanctuary of Humanity, please contact the Salt Monument:

P. O. Box 1542, Boulder, CO 80306
email: SaltMonument@hotmail.com